Eng.d by A.H. Ritchie.

John Bright

SPEECHES

OF

JOHN BRIGHT, M. P.

ON THE

AMERICAN QUESTION.

WITH AN INTRODUCTION

BY FRANK MOORE.

BOSTON:
LITTLE, BROWN, AND COMPANY.
1865.

UNIVERSITY PRESS: WELCH, BIGELOW, & CO.,
CAMBRIDGE.

CONTENTS.

Contents.

INTRODUCTION.

John Bright, one of the most active, intelligent, and liberal of those in Europe who have become identified with the recent history of events in America, was born on the 16th of November, 1811, at Greenbank, Rochdale, England, the residence of his father, Jacob Bright, a cotton spinner and manufacturer. He received an ordinary school education, and at the age of fifteen was placed in the counting-house of his father, to be instructed in the details and management of the business, — destined to become his by inheritance, his elder brother having died at an early age. To the acquirement of this knowledge he earnestly devoted himself until 1835, when he found time to enlarge his sphere of observation and study by a visit to the Continent, where he passed several months, extending his travels through Egypt and the Holy Land.

Three years later, in 1838, he entered upon his public career, as a member of the Anti-Corn-Law League. In this organization he became intimately associated with Richard Cobden, and with him labored in the cause of political reform with such zeal and persistence that the result thus achieved has passed into history. He astonished and delighted those by whom he was surrounded with the clearness of his political views, which were developed with remarkable perspicuity and advocated with all the powers of a splendid eloquence. "While Mr. Cobden lent his calm and unanswerable logic to the cause," says a contemporary, "Mr. Bright gave it the impetus of zeal and passion. The one sapped the foundations of economic error, the other battered at its walls. The one convinced his opponents, the other carried them away captive; and both rendered such efficient service as to make it difficult to say which was the most useful or the most powerful. Public meetings were held in every part of the British kingdom; newspapers were established in the interest of the agitation; wherever there was a possibility of success, the country was deluged with pamphlets; eminent men entered the ranks, but towering high above them all were the names of Cobden and Bright. The speeches of the latter were of the most effective description, and thoroughly English in manner as well as in phraseology. Powerful and impassioned, he so won his auditors that even those who opposed his theories were compelled to admire his genius."

The League lost no opportunity to advance the interests of so able a champion, and in 1843, a vacancy having occurred, Mr. Bright contested the representation of the city of Durham in Parliament. In this first attempt he was defeated, but in the same year, his opponent having been unseated for bribery, he was successful, and entered the House of Commons, where he again joined hands with Mr. Cobden, who had been returned for Stockport two years earlier.

Mr. Bright was a Radical and Free Trade Reformer, attached to no political party, but willing to support either, provided their principles and measures were "founded upon the wants of the country and the rights of the people." The leading object of his political life, however, was the repeal of the Corn Laws. He continued to represent Durham until after the attainment of this object, and the consequent establishment of the Free Trade policy of the British empire.

Soon after this, Mr. Bright became the candidate for Manchester, and, although many were opposed to his claims, he was triumphantly elected by a coalition of the Free Trade and the Ultra-Liberal parties. From this time his activity in Parliament and on the platform was varied and continuous.

In the House of Commons he proposed the application of the principle of Free Trade to transactions in land, as a remedy for the suffering and oppression which produced the Irish famine. He pleaded unsuccessfully for the appointment of a Royal Commission to investigate the condition of affairs in India, and in 1849 he was appointed a member of the Select Committee of the House of Commons on Official Salaries. He co-operated with Mr. Cobden in his financial reform movement; and in 1851 he became identified with the party in Parliament who desired to censure Lord Palmerston for his conduct towards the government of Greece in the matter of the claims of Don Pacifico. During the next year he assisted at the reception of Kossuth by the Liberals at Manchester.

At the general election which followed the reorganization of the Anti-Corn-Law League, Mr. Bright, notwithstanding a strenuous opposition, was re-elected by a considerable majority. He continued in Parliament until 1857, when, owing to his course in reference to Lord Palmerston and the Chinese War, he lost his seat. But his absence from Parliament was of short duration, as in the autumn of the same year he was returned as the representative from Birmingham. During the years 1858 and 1859, he made a tour of the Provinces, and published an elaborate scheme of changes in the representative system of Great Britain. In 1860 he lent his ardent support to the Reform Bill introduced into the House of Commons by Lord John Russell.

Mr. Bright was ever a sincere friend to the United States, and often bestowed unstinted praise upon the institutions of this country. A zealous advocate of freedom and the education of the people, he clearly saw the advantages to be derived from free labor, and rightly estimated the vast benefits arising from public schools. At the breaking out of the Southern Rebellion, foreseeing that the contest was not alone for the perpetuation of liberal institutions and the maintenance of the government, but that it was to be the death-struggle between Freedom and Slavery, he unhesitatingly and unreservedly sided with the North, and was largely instrumental in presenting the Union cause in its true light to the government and the people of Great Britain.

Extensively engaged in the manufacture of cotton,—with his business seriously affected, therefore, by the limited supply of that staple,—he was yet too thoroughly attached to principles he had early espoused and had always supported, to give any countenance to those who strove to entangle the two nations in a war tending to advance the interests of the South. "If all other tongues are silent," said he, "mine shall speak for that policy which gives hope to the bondsmen of the South, and which tends to generous thoughts and generous words and generous deeds between the two great nations who speak the English language, and from their origin are alike entitled to the English name."

During the suffering and consequent excitement in Lancashire, occasioned by the stopping of the mills, Mr. Bright addressed numerous meetings of workingmen, and, in a series of masterly and convincing speeches, thoroughly refuted the statements of Southern sympathizers, and re-established the kindly feelings which found expression in the "Address of the Trades' Unions and Workingmen of England to President Lincoln." It will not be out of place to ask attention to the opinions of Mr. Bright upon the production of cotton, embodied in these addresses. The result of years of practical experience and careful observation, these expositions of the views of one who discusses the subject, not only in its relations to his particular business, but in its multiform bearings upon free labor, upon the social advancement of the workingman, and its political significance to a great nation, deserve the careful consideration of merchants and statesmen.

During the darkest hours of the Rebellion Mr. Bright remained hopeful, believing that the destinies of the Republic were in the hands of God. Addressing the workingmen in February, 1863, he says: —

"I advise you not to believe in the 'destruction' of the American nation. If facts should happen by any chance to force you to believe it, don't commit the crime of wishing it. . . . . From the very outburst of this great convulsion, I have had but one hope and one faith, and it was this: that the result of this stupendous strife might be to make freedom the heritage forever of a whole continent, and that the grandeur and the prosperity of the American Union might never be impaired."

And in June, 1863, after the disaster at Chancellorsville, and before the success at Gettysburg, he closes a speech, in reply to

Mr. Roebuck's motion for the recognition of the Southern Confederacy, in these words: "We know the cause of this revolt, its purposes and its aims. Those who made it have not left us in darkness respecting their intentions, but what they are to accomplish is still hidden from our sight. . . . . Whether it will give freedom to the race which white men have trampled in the dust, or whether the issue will purify a nation steeped in crime in connection with its conduct to that race, is known only to the Supreme. In his hand are alike the breath of man and the life of states. I am willing to commit to Him the issue of this dreaded contest; but I implore of Him, and I beseech this House, that my country may lift nor hand nor voice in aid of the most stupendous act of guilt that history has recorded in the annals of mankind."

The course of Mr. Bright, in Parliament and among the people, on the great questions in American politics, demands the gratitude of civilized nations. Firmly grounded in the principles of right and justice, he has never deviated from the path which his ripe judgment led him to choose at the commencement of the Rebellion; and future generations of Americans will remember his exertions in their behalf with the deepest affection and regard, while his honesty and persistence in the great cause of human rights will call down upon him the admiration of the liberty-loving men of all lands.

The Speeches embraced in the following pages were revised and corrected by Mr. Bright, and they are now presented to the American public with his approbation.

New York, June, 1865.

JOHN BRIGHT

ON THE AMERICAN QUESTION.

Extract from a Speech delivered at a Meeting at Rochdale, to promote the Election of John Cheetham, Esq. for the Southern Division of the County of Lancaster, August 1, 1861.

Mr. Bright said: —

I think that, just now, if you can find a man who on questions of great state policy agrees with us, at the same time having a deep personal interest in this great cotton question, and having paid so much attention to it as Mr. Cheetham has, — I think there is a double reason why he should receive the votes and have the confidence of this division of the county. (Cheers.) Now, is this cotton question a great question or not? I met a spinner to-day, — he does not live in Rochdale, though I met him here, — and I asked him what he thought about it; and he said, "Well, I think cotton will come somehow." (Laughter.) And I find that there is that kind of answer to be had from three out of four of all the spinners that you ask. They know that in past times, when cotton has risen fifty or eighty per cent, or some extravagant rise, something has come,—the rate of interest has been raised, or there has been a commercial panic from some cause or other, and down the price has gone; and when everybody said, "There would be no cotton at Christmas," there proved a very considerable stock at Christmas. And so they say now.

I don't in the least deny that it will be so; all I assert is, that this particular case is new, that we have never had a war in the United States between different sections of that country, affecting the production of cotton before; and it is not fair, or wise, but rather childish than otherwise, to argue from past events, which were not a bit like this, of the event which is now passing before our eyes. They say, "It is quite true there is a civil war in America, but it will blow over: there will be a compromise; or the English government will break the blockade." Now recollect what breaking the blockade means. It means a war with the United States; and I don't think that it would be cheap to break the blockade at the cost of a war with the United States. I think that the cost of a war with the United States would give probably half wages, for a very considerable time, to those persons in Lancashire who would be out of work if there was no cotton, to say nothing at all of the manifest injustice and wrong against all international law, that a legal and effective blockade should be interfered with by another country.

It is not exactly the business of this meeting, but my opinion is, that the safety of the product on which this county depends rests far more on the success of the Washington government than upon its failure; and I believe nothing could be more monstrous than for us, who are not very averse to war ourselves, to set up for critics, carping, cavilling critics, of what the Washington government is doing. I saw a letter the other day from an Englishman, resident for twenty-five years in Philadelphia, a merchant there, and a very prosperous merchant. He said, "I prefer the institutions of this country (the United States) very much to yours in England"; but he says also, "If it be once admitted that here we have no country and no government, but that any portion of these United States can break off from the central government whenever it pleases, then it is time for me to pack up what I have, and to go somewhere where there is a country and a government."

Well, that is the pith of this question. Do you suppose that, if Lancashire and Yorkshire thought that they would break off from the United Kingdom, those newspapers which are now preaching every kind of moderation to the government of Washington would advise the government in London to allow these two counties to set up a special government for themselves? When the people in Ireland wished to secede, was it proposed in London that they should be allowed to secede peaceably? Nothing of the kind. I am not going to defend what is taking place in a country that is well able to defend itself. But I advise you, and I advise the people of England, to abstain from applying to the United States doctrines and principles which we never apply to our own case. At any rate, they have never fought "for the balance of power" in Europe. They have never fought to keep up a decaying empire. They have never squandered the money of their people in such phantom expeditions as we have been engaged in. And now at this moment, when you are told that they are going to be ruined by their vast expenditure, the sum that they are now going to raise in the great emergency of this grievous war is no greater than what we raise every year during a time of peace. (Loud cheers.) They say that they are not going to liberate slaves. No; the object of the Washington government is to maintain their own Constitution, and to act legally, as it permits and requires.

No man is more in favor of peace than I am; no man has denounced war more than I have, probably, in this country; few men, in their public life, have suffered more obloquy — I had almost said, more indignity — in consequence of it. But I cannot, for the life of me, see, upon any of those principles upon which states are governed now, — I say nothing of the literal word of the New Testament, — I cannot see how the state of affairs in America, with regard to the United States government, could have been different from what it is at this moment. We had a heptarchy in this country, and it was thought to be a good thing to get rid of it, and to have a united nation. If the thirty-three or thirty-four States of the American Union can break off whenever they like, I can see nothing but disaster and confusion throughout the whole of that continent. I say that the war, be it successful or not, be it Christian or not, be it wise or not, is a war to sustain the government and to sustain the authority of a great nation; and that the people of England, if they are true to their own sympathies, to their own history, and to their own great act of 1834, to which reference has already been made, will have no sympathy with those who wish to build up a great empire on the perpetual bondage of millions of their fellow-men. (Loud cheers.)

SPEECH AT A DINNER AT ROCHDALE,

DECEMBER 4, 1861.

Delivered during the Excitement caused by the Seizure of Mason and Slidell on Board the "Trent" Steamer.

Mr. Bright, who was received with tumultuous cheering and waving of handkerchiefs, rose and said: —

When the gentlemen who invited me to this dinner called upon me, I felt their kindness very sensibly, and now I am deeply grateful to my friends around me, and to you all, for the abundant manifestations of kindness with which I have been received to-night. I am, as you all know, surrounded at this moment by my neighbors and friends, (Hear! Hear!) and I may say with the utmost truth, that I value the good opinions of those who now hear my voice far beyond the opinions of any equal number of the inhabitants of this country selected from any other portion of it. You have, by this act of kindness that you have shown me, given proof that in the main you do not disapprove of my course and labors, — (Cheers,) — that at least you are willing to express an opinion that the motives by which I have been actuated have been honest and honorable to myself, and that that course has not been entirely without service to my country. (Applause.) Coming to this meeting, or to any similar meeting, I always find that the subjects for discussion appear too many, and far more than it is possible to treat. In these times in which we live, by the influence of the telegraph, and the steamboat, and the railroad, and the multiplication of newspapers, we seem continually to stand as on the top of an exceeding high mountain, from which we behold all the kingdoms of the earth and all the glory of them, — unhappily, also, not only their glory, but their crimes, and their follies, and their calamities.

Seven years ago, our eyes were turned with

anxious expectation to a remote corner of Europe, where five nations were contending in bloody strife for an object which possibly hardly one of them comprehended, and, if they did comprehend it, which all sensible men amongst them must have known to be absolutely impracticable. Four years ago, we were looking still farther to the East, where there was a gigantic revolt in a great dependency of the British Crown, arising mainly from gross neglect, and from the incapacity of England, up to that moment, to govern the country which it had known how to conquer. Two years ago, we looked south, to the plains of Lombardy, and saw a great strife there, in which every man in England took a strong interest;—(Hear! Hear!)—and we have welcomed, as the result of that strife, the addition of a great kingdom to the list of European states. (Cheers.) Now, our eyes are turned in a contrary direction, and we look to the West. There we see a struggle in progress of the very highest interest to England and to humanity at large. We see there a nation whom I shall call the Transatlantic English nation, — (Hear! Hear!) — the inheritor and partaker of all the historic glories of this country. We see it torn with intestine broils, and suffering from calamities from which for more than a century past — in fact, for more than two centuries past — this country has been exempt. That struggle is of especial interest to us. We remember the description which one of our great poets gives of Rome, —

"Lone mother of dead empires."

But England is the living mother of great nations on the American and on the Australian continents, which promise to endow the world with all our knowledge and all our civilization, and even something more than the freedom she herself enjoys. (Cheers.)

Eighty-five years ago, at the time when some of our oldest townsmen were very little children, there were, on the North American continent, Colonies, mainly of Englishmen, containing about three millions of souls. These Colonies we have seen a year ago constituting the United States of North America, and comprising a population of no less than thirty millions of souls. We know that in agriculture and manufactures, with the exception of this kingdom, there is no country in the world which in these arts may be placed in advance of the United States. (Applause.) With regard to inventions, I believe, within the last thirty years, we have received more useful inventions from the United States than we have received from all the other countries of the earth. (Hear! Hear!) In that country there are probably ten times as many miles of telegraph as there are in this country, and there are at least five or six times as many miles of railway. The tonnage of its shipping is at least equal to ours, if it does not exceed ours. The prisons of that country — for, even in countries the most favored, prisons are needful — have been models for other nations of the earth; and many European governments have sent missions at different times to inquire into the admirable system of education so universally adopted in their free schools throughout the Northern States.

If I were to speak of this country in a religious aspect, I should say that, considering the short space of time to which their history goes back, there is nothing on the face of the earth besides, and never has been, to equal the magnificent arrangement of churches and ministers, and of all the appliances which are thought necessary for a nation to teach Christianity and morality to its people. (Cheers.) Besides all this, when I state that for many years past the annual public expenditure of the government of that country has been somewhere between £10,000,000 and £15,000,000, I need not perhaps say further, that there has always existed amongst all the population an amount of comfort and prosperity and abounding plenty such as I believe no other country in the world, in any age, has displayed. (Applause.)

This is a very fine, but a very true picture; yet it has another side to which I must advert. There has been one great feature in that country, one great contrast, which has been pointed to by all who have commented upon the United States as a feature of danger and contrast calculated to give pain. You have had in that country the utmost liberty to the white man, and bondage and degradation to the black man. Now rely upon it, that wherever Christianity lives and flourishes, there must grow up from it necessarily a conscience hostile to any oppression and to any wrong; and therefore, from the hour when the United States Constitution was formed, so long as it left there this great evil, — then comparatively small, but now so great, — it left there seeds of that which an American statesman has so happily described, of that "irrepressible conflict" of which now the whole world is the witness. It has been a common thing for men disposed to carp at the United States to point at this blot upon their fair fame, and to compare it with the boasted declaration of freedom in their deed and Declaration of Independence. But we must recollect who sowed this seed of trouble, and how and by whom it has been cherished.

Without dwelling upon this stain any longer, I should like to read to you a paragraph from the instructions supposed to be given to the Virginia delegates to Congress, in the month of August, 1774, by Mr. Jefferson, who was perhaps the ablest man the United States had produced up to that time, and who was then actively engaged in its affairs, and afterwards for two periods filled the office of President. He represents this very Slave State, — the State of Virginia, — and he says: —

"For the most trifling reasons, and sometimes for no conceivable reason at all, his Majesty has rejected laws of the most salutary tendency. The abolition of domestic slavery is the great object of desire in those Colonies where it was unhappily introduced in their infant state. But previous to the enfranchisement of the slaves we have, it is necessary to exclude all further importations from Africa. Yet our repeated attempts to effect this by prohibition, and by imposing duties which might amount to prohibition, have hitherto been defeated by his Majesty's negative, — thus preferring the immediate advantages of a few British corsairs to the lasting interests of the American States, and to the rights of human nature, deeply wounded by this infamous practice."

I read this merely to show that, two years before the Declaration of Independence was signed, Mr. Jefferson, acting on behalf of those he represented in Virginia, read that protest against the course of the English government which prevented the Colonists abolishing the slave-trade, preparatory to the abolition of slavery itself.

Well, the United States Constitution left the slave question for every State to manage for itself. It was a question too difficult to settle then, and apparently every man had the hope and belief that in a few years slavery in itself would become extinct. Then there happened a great event in the annals of manufactures and commerce. It was discovered that in those States that article which we in this county now so much depend on could be produced of the best quality necessary for manufacture, and at a moderate price. From that day to this the growth of cotton has increased there, and its consumption has increased here, and a value which no man dreamed of when Jefferson wrote that paper has been given the slave and to slave industry. Thus it has grown up to that gigantic institution which now threatens either its own overthrow or the overthrow of that which is a million times more valuable, — the United States of America. (Cheers.)

The crisis to which we have arrived, — I say "we," for after all we are nearly as much interested as if I was making this speech in the city of Boston or the city of New York, —

the crisis, I say, which has now arrived, was inevitable. I say that the conscience of the North, never satisfied with the institution of slavery, was constantly urging some men forward to take a more extreme view of the question; and there grew up naturally a section — it may be not a very numerous one — in favor of the abolition of slavery. A great and powerful party resolved at least upon a restraint and a control of slavery, so that it should not extend beyond the States and the area which it now occupies. But, if we look at the government of the United States almost ever since the formation of the Union, we shall find the Southern power has been mostly dominant there. If we take thirty-six years after the formation of the present Constitution,— I think about 1787,—we shall find that for thirty-two of those years every President was a Southern man; and if we take the period from 1828 until 1860, we shall find on every election for President the South voted in the majority.

We know what an election is in the United States for President of the Republic. There is a most extensive suffrage, and there is the ballot-box. The members of the House of Representatives are elected by the same suffrage, and generally they are elected at the same time. It is thus therefore almost inevitable that the House of Representatives is in accord in public policy with the President for the time being. Every four years there springs from the vote created by the whole people a President over that great nation. I think the world offers no finer spectacle than this; it offers no higher dignity; and there is no greater object of ambition on the political stage on which men are permitted to move. You may point, if you will, to hereditary rulers, to crowns coming down through successive generations of the same family, to thrones based on prescription or on conquest, to sceptres wielded over veteran legions and subject realms, — but to my mind there is nothing so worthy of reverence and obedience, and nothing more sacred, than the authority of the freely chosen by the majority of a great and free people (applause); and if there be on earth and amongst men any right divine to govern, surely it rests with a ruler so chosen and so appointed. (Renewed applause.)

Last year the ceremony of this great election was gone through, and the South, which had been so long successful, found itself defeated. That defeat was followed instantly by secession, and insurrection, and war. In the multitude of articles which have been before us in the newspapers within the last few months, I have no doubt you have seen it stated, as I have seen it, that this question was very much like that upon which the Colonies originally revolted against the Crown of England. It is amazing how little some newspaper writers know, or how little they think you know. ("Hear!" and laughter.) When the war of independence was begun in America, ninety years ago, there were no representatives there at all. The question then was, whether a ministry in Downing Street, and a corrupt and borough-mongering Parliament, should continue to impose taxes upon three millions of English subjects, who had left their native shores and established themselves in North America. But now the question is not the want of representation, because, as is perfectly notorious, the South is not only represented, but is represented in excess; for, in distributing the number of representatives, which is done every ten years, three out of every five slaves are counted as freemen, and the number of representatives from the Slave States is consequently so much greater than if the freemen, the white men only, were counted. From this cause the Southern States have twenty members more in the House of Representatives than they would have if the members were apportioned on the same principle as in the Northern Free States. Therefore you will see at once that there is no comparison between the state of things when the Colonies revolted, and the state of things now, when this wicked insurrection has broken out.

There is another cause which is sometimes in England assigned for this great misfortune, which is, the protective theories in operation in the Union, and the maintenance of a high tariff. It happens with regard to that, unfortunately, that no American, certainly no one I ever met with, attributed the disasters of the Union to that cause. It is an argument made use of by ignorant Englishmen, but never by informed Americans. (Hear! Hear!) I have already shown you that the South, during almost the whole existence of the Union, has been dominant at Washington; and during that period the tariff has existed, and there has been no general dissatisfaction with it. Occasionally, there can be no doubt, their tariff was higher than was thought just or reasonable or necessary by some of the States of the South.

But the first act of the United States which levies duties upon imports, passed immediately after the Union was formed, recites that "It is necessary for the encouragement and protection of manufactures to levy the duties which follow"; and during the war with England from 1812 to 1815, the people of the United States had to pay for all the articles they brought from Europe many times over the natural cost of those articles, on account of the interruption to the traffic by the English nation.

When the war was over, it was felt by everybody desirable that they should encourage manufacturers in their own country; and seeing that England at the precise moment was passing a law to prevent any wheat coming from America until wheat in England had risen to the price of 84*s.* per quarter, we may be quite satisfied that the doctrine of protection originally entertained did not find less favor at the close of the war in 1815. (Hear! Hear!)

There is one remarkable point with regard to this matter which should not be forgotten. Twelve months ago, at the meeting of the Congress of the United States, on the first Monday in December, — when the Congress met, you recollect that there were various propositions of compromise, committee meetings of various kinds to try and devise some mode of settling the question between the North and the South, so that disunion might not go on, — though I read carefully everything published in the English papers from the United States on the subject, I do not recollect that in a single instance the question of the tariff was referred to, or any change proposed or suggested in the matter as likely to have any effect whatever upon the question of Secession.

There is another point, that whatever might be the influence of the tariff upon the United States, it is as pernicious to the West as it is to the South; and further, that Louisiana, which is a Southern State and a seceded State, has always voted along with Pennsylvania until last year in favor of protection, — protection for its sugar, whilst Pennsylvania wished protection for its coal and iron. But if the tariff was onerous and grievous, was that any reason for this great insurrection? Was there ever a country that had a tariff, especially in the article of food, more onerous and more cruel than that which we had in this country twenty years ago? (Cheers.) We did not secede. We did not rebel. What we did was to raise money for the purpose of distributing among all the people perfect information upon the question; and many men, as you know, devoted all their labors, for several years, to teach the great and wise doctrine of free trade to the people of England. (Cheers.) Why, the price of a single gunboat, the equipment of a single regiment, the garrisoning of a single fort, the cessation of their trade for a single day, cost more than it would have cost to have spread among all the intelligent people of the United States the most complete statement of the whole case; and the West and South could easily have revised, or, if need had been, have repealed the tariff altogether. (Cheers.)

The question is a very different and a far more grave question. It is a question of slavery, — (Cheers,) — and for thirty years it has constantly been coming to the surface, disturbing social life, and overthrowing almost all political harmony in the working of the United States. (Cheers.) In the North there is no secession; there is no collision. These disturbances and this insurrection are found wholly in the South and in the Slave States; and therefore I think that the man who says otherwise, who contends that it is the tariff, or anything whatsoever else than slavery, is either himself deceived or endeavors to deceive others. (Cheers.) The object of the South is this, to escape from the majority who wish to limit the area of slavery. (Hear! Hear!) They wish to found a Slave State freed from the influence and the opinions of freedom. The Free States in the North now stand before the world the advocates and defenders of freedom and civilization. The Slave States offer themselves for the recognition of a Christian nation, based upon the foundation, the unchangeable foundation in their eyes, of slavery and barbarism. (Cheers.)

I will not discuss the guilt of the men who, ministers of a great nation only last year, conspired to overthrow it. I will not point out or recapitulate the statements of the fraudulent manner in which they disposed of the funds in the national exchequer. I will not point out by name any of the men, in this conspiracy, whom history will designate by titles they would not like to hear; but I say that slavery has sought to break up the most free government in the world, and to found a new state, in the nineteenth century, whose corner-stone is the perpetual bondage of millions of men. (Loud applause.)

Well now, having thus described what appears to me briefly the literal truth of this matter, what is the course that England would be expected to pursue? We should be neutral so far as regards mingling in the strife. (Cheers.) We were neutral in the strife in Italy; but we were not neutral in opinion or sympathy; and we know perfectly well that throughout the whole of Italy at this moment there is a feeling that, though no shot was fired from an English ship, and though no English soldier trod their soil, yet still the opinion of England was potent in Europe, and did much for the creation of the Italian kingdom. (Cheers.)

Well, with regard to the United States, you know how much we hate slavery, — that is, awhile ago we thought we knew; that we have given twenty millions sterling, — a million a year, or nearly so, of taxes forever, — to free eight hundred thousand slaves in the

English colonies. We knew, or thought we knew, how much we were in love with free government everywhere, although it might not take precisely the same form as our own government. We were for free government in Italy; we were for free government in Switzerland; and we were for free government, even under a republican form, in the United States of America; and with all this, every man would have said that England would wish the American Union to be prosperous and eternal.

Now, suppose we turn our eyes to the East, to the empire of Russia, for a moment. In Russia, as you all know, there has been one of the most important and magnificent changes of policy ever seen in any country. Within the last year or two, the present Emperor of Russia, following the wishes of his father, has insisted upon the abolition of serfdom in that empire; and twenty-three millions of human beings, lately serfs, little better than real slaves, have been raised to the ranks of freedom. (Cheers.) Now, suppose that the millions of the serfs of Russia had been chiefly in the South of Russia. We hear of the nobles of Russia, to whom those serfs belonged in a great measure, that they have been hostile to this change; and there has been some danger that the peace of that empire might be disturbed during the change. Suppose these nobles, for the purpose of maintaining in perpetuity the serfdom of Russia, and barring out twenty-three millions of your fellow-creatures from the rights of freedom, had established a great and secret conspiracy, and that they had risen in great and dangerous insurrection against the Russian government, — I say that you, the people of England, although seven years ago you were in mortal combat with the Russians in the South of Europe, — I believe at this moment you would have prayed Heaven in all sincerity and fervor to give strength to the arm and success to the great wishes of the Emperor, and that the vile and atrocious insurrection might be suppressed. (Cheers.)

Well, but let us look a little at what has been said and done in this country since the period when Parliament rose at the beginning of August. There have been two speeches to which I wish to refer, and in terms of approbation. The Duke of Argyll, a member of the present government, — and, though I have not the smallest personal acquaintance with him, I am free to say that I believe him one of the most intelligent and liberal of his order, — the Duke of Argyll made a speech which was fair and friendly to the government of the United States. Lord Stanley, only a fortnight ago I think, made a speech which it is impossible to read without remarking the thought, the liberality, and the wisdom by which it is distinguished. He doubted, it is true, whether the Union could be restored. A man need not be hostile, and must not necessarily be unfriendly, to doubt that or the contrary; but he spoke with fairness and friendliness of the government of the United States; and he said that they were right and justifiable in the course they took; and he gave a piece of advice, — which is now more important than at the moment when it was given, — that, amid the various incidents and accidents of a struggle of this nature, it became a people like this to be very moderate, very calm, and to avoid getting into any feeling of irritation, which sometimes arises, and sometimes leads to danger. (Hear! Hear!)

I mention these two speeches as from Englishmen of great distinction in this country, speeches which I believe will have a beneficial effect on the other side of the Atlantic. (Cheers.) Lord John Russell, in the House of Commons, during the last session, made a speech too, in which he rebuked the impertinence of a young member of the House who had spoken about the bursting of the "bubble republic." It was a speech worthy of the best days of Lord John Russell.

(Cheers.) But at a later period he spoke at Newcastle on an occasion something like this, when the inhabitants, or some portion of the inhabitants, of the town invited him to a public dinner. He described the contest in words something like this, — I speak from memory only: The North is contending for empire, the South for independence. Did he mean contending for empire, as England when making some fresh conquest in India? If he meant that, what he said was not true. (Cheers.) But I recollect Lord John Russell, some years ago, in the House of Commons, on an occasion when I made some observation as to the unreasonable expenditure of our colonies, and said that the people of England should not be taxed to defray expenses which the colonies themselves were well able to bear, turned to me with a sharpness which was not necessary, and said, "The honorable member has no objection to make a great empire into a small one; but I have." (Cheers.) Perhaps if he had lived in the United States, if he was a member of the Senate or the House of Representatives there, he would doubt whether it was his duty to consent at once to the destruction of a great country by separation, it may be into two hostile camps, or whether he would not try all the means which were open to him, and would be open to the government, to avert so unlooked for and so dire a calamity. (Cheers.)

There are other speeches that have been made. I will not refer to them by any quotation, — I will not out of pity to some of the men who uttered them. (Laughter.) I will not bring their names even before you, to give them an endurance which I hope they will not otherwise obtain. I leave them in the obscurity which they so richly merit. But you know as well as I do, that, of all the speeches made since the end of the last session of Parliament by public men, by politicians, the majority of them have either displayed a strange ignorance of American affairs, or a stranger absence of that cordiality and friendship which, I maintain, our American kinsmen have a right to look for at our hands.

And if we part from the speakers and turn to the writers, what do we find there? We find that which is reputed abroad, and has hitherto been believed in at home, as the most powerful representative of English opinion, — at least of the richer classes, — we find in that particular newspaper there has not been since Mr. Lincoln took office, in March last, as President of the United States, one fair and honorable and friendly article on American affairs in the columns of that paper. (Cheers.) Some of you, I dare say, read it; but, fortunately, every district is now so admirably supplied with local newspapers, that I trust in all time to come the people of England will drink of purer streams nearer home, — (Cheers,) — and not of those streams which are muddled by party feeling and political intrigue, and by many motives that tend to anything rather than the enlightenment and advantage of the people. (Cheers.) It is said, — that very paper has said over and over again, — "Why this war? Why not separate peaceably? Why this fratricidal strife?" I hope it is equally averse to fratricidal strife in other districts; for if it be true that God made of one blood all the families of man to dwell on the face of all the earth, it must be fratricidal strife whether we are slaughtering Russians in the Crimea or bombarding towns on the sea-coast of the United States. (Cheers.)

Now no one will expect that I should stand forward as the advocate of war, or as the defender of that great sum of all crimes which is involved in war. But when we are discussing a question of this nature, it is only fair that we should discuss it upon principles which are acknowledged not only in the country where the strife is being carried on, but are universally acknowledged in this country. When I discussed the Russian war, seven or eight years ago, I always disavowed it, on principles which were avowed by the government and people of England, and I took my facts from the blue-books presented to Parliament. (Cheers.) I take the liberty, then, of doing that in this case; and I say that, looking at the principles avowed in England, and at its policy, there is no man, who is not absolutely a non-resistant in every sense, who can fairly challenge the conduct of the American government in this war. (Loud cheers.) It would be a curious thing to find that the party in this country which on every public question is in favor of war at any cost, when they come to speak of the duty of the government of the United States, is in favor "of peace at any price." (Laughter.)

I want to know whether it has ever been admitted by politicians, or statesmen, or people, that a great nation can be broken up at any time by any particular section of any part of that nation. It has been tried occasionally in Ireland, and if it had succeeded history would have said that it was with very good cause. But if anybody tried now to get up a secession or insurrection in Ireland, — and it would be infinitely less disturbing to everything than the secession in the United States, because there is a boundary which nobody can dispute, — I am quite sure the *Times* would have its "special correspondent," and would describe with all the glee and exultation in the world the manner in which the Irish insurrectionists were cut down and made an end of. (Cheers.)

Let any man try in this country to restore the heptarchy, do you think that any portion of the people would think that the thing could be tolerated for a moment? But if you would look at a map of the United States, you would see there is no country in the world probably, at this moment, where any plan of separation between the North and the South, as far as the question of boundary is concerned, is so surrounded with insurmountable difficulties. For example, Maryland is a Slave State; but Maryland, by a large majority, voted for the Union. Kentucky is a Slave State, one of the finest in the Union, and containing a fine people; Kentucky has voted for the Union, but has been invaded from the South. Missouri is a Slave State; but Missouri has not seceded, and has been invaded by the South, and there is a secession party in that State. There are parts of Virginia which have formed themselves into a new State, resolved to adhere to the North; and there is no doubt a considerable Northern and Union feeling in the State of Tennessee. I have no doubt there is in every other State. In fact, I am not sure that there is not now within sound of my voice a citizen of the State of Alabama, who would tell you that there the question of secession has never been put to the vote; and that there are great numbers of men, reasonable and thoughtful and just men, in that State, who entirely deplore the condition of things there existing.

Then, what would you do with all those States, and with what we may call the loyal portion of the people of those States? Would you allow them to be dragooned into this insurrection, and into the formation or the becoming parts of a new State, to which they themselves are hostile? And what would you do with the city of Washington? Washington is in a Slave State. Would anybody have advised that President Lincoln and his Cabinet, with all the members of Congress, of the House of Representatives and the Senate, from the North, with their wives and children, and everybody else who was not positively in favor of the South, should have set off on their melancholy pilgrimage northwards, leaving that capital, hallowed to them by such associations, — having its name even from the father of their country, — leaving Washington to the South, because Washington is situated in a Slave State?

Again, what do you say to the Mississippi

River, as you see it upon the map, the "father of waters," rolling that gigantic stream to the ocean? Do you think that the fifty millions which one day will occupy the banks of that river northward, will ever consent that that great stream should roll through a foreign, and it may be a hostile State? And more, there are four millions of negroes in subjection. For them the American Union is directly responsible. They are not Secessionists; they are now, as they always were, not citizens nor subjects, but legally under the care and power of the government of the United States. Would you consent that these should be delivered up to the tender mercies of their task-masters, the defenders of slavery as an everlasting institution? (Cheers.)

Well, if all had been surrendered without a struggle, what then? What would the writers in this newspaper and other newspapers have said? If a bare rock in your empire, that would not keep a goat — a single goat — alive, be touched by any foreign power, the whole empire is roused to resistance; and if there be, from accident or passion, the smallest insult to your flag, what do your newspaper writers say upon the subject, and what is said in all your towns and upon all your exchanges? I will tell you what they would have said if the government of the Northern States had taken their insidious and dishonest advice. They would have said the great Republic was a failure, that democracy had murdered patriotism, that history afforded no example of such meanness and of such cowardice; and they would have heaped unmeasured obloquy and contempt upon the people and government who had taken that course. (Loud cheers.)

Well, they tell you, these candid friends of the United States, — they tell you that all freedom is gone; that the Habeas Corpus Act, if they ever had one, is known no longer; and that any man may be arrested at the dictum of the President or of the Secretary of State. Well, but in 1848 you recollect, many of you, that there was a small insurrection in Ireland. It was an absurd thing altogether; but what was done then? I saw, in one night, in the House of Commons, a bill for the suspension of the Habeas Corpus Act passed through all its stages. What more did I see? I saw a bill brought in by the Whig government of that day, Lord John Russell being the premier, which made speaking against the government and against the crown — which up to that time had been sedition — which proposed to make it felony; and it was only by the greatest exertions of a few of the members that that act, in that particular, was limited to a period of two years. In the same session a bill was brought in called an Alien Bill, which enabled the Home Secretary to take any foreigner whatsoever, not being a naturalized Englishman, and in twenty-four hours to send him out of the country. Although a man might have committed no crime, this might be done to him, apparently only on suspicion.

But suppose that an insurgent army had been so near to London that you could see its outposts from every suburb of London, what then do you think would have been the regard of the government of Great Britain for personal liberty, if it interfered with the necessities, and, as they might think, the salvation of the state? I recollect, in 1848, when the Habeas Corpus Act was suspended, that a number of persons in Liverpool, men there of position and of wealth, presented a petition to the House of Commons, praying — what? That the Habeas Corpus Act should not be suspended? No. They were not content with its suspension in Ireland; but they prayed the House of Commons to extend that suspension to Liverpool. (Laughter.) I recollect that at that time — and I am sure my friend Mr. Wilson will bear me out in what I say — the Mayor of Liverpool telegraphed with the Mayor of Manchester, and that messages were sent on to London nearly every hour. The Mayor of Manchester heard from the Mayor of Liverpool that certain Irishmen in Liverpool, conspirators, or fellow-conspirators with those in Ireland, were going to burn the cotton warehouses in Liverpool and the cotton mills of Lancashire. (Laughter.) And I read that petition. I took it from the table of the House of Commons, and read it, and I handed it over to a statesman of great eminence, who has been but just removed from us, — I refer to Sir James Graham, — (Hear! Hear!) — a man not second to any in the House of Commons for his knowledge of affairs and for his great capacity, — I handed to him this petition. He read it; and after he had read it, he rose from his seat, and laid it upon the table with a gesture of abhorrence and disgust. (Loud cheers.) Now that was a petition from the town of Liverpool, in which some persons have been making themselves very ridiculous of late by reason of their conduct. (Hear! Hear!)

There is one more point. It has been said, "How much better it would be" — not for the United States, but — "for us, that these States should be divided." I recollect meeting a gentleman in Bond Street one day before the session was over. He was a rich man, and one whose voice is very much heard in the House of Commons; but his voice is not heard there when he is on his legs, but when he is cheering other speakers (laughter); and he said to me: "After all, this is a sad business about the United States; but still I think it is very much better that they should be split up. In twenty years," or in fifty years, I forget which it was, "they will be so powerful that they will bully all Europe." And a distinguished member of the House of Commons, — distinguished there by his eloquence, distinguished more by his many writings, — I mean Sir Edward Bulwer Lytton, — he did not exactly express a hope, but he ventured on something like a prediction, that the time would come when there would be, I don't know how many, but as many independent States in America as you can count upon your fingers.

There cannot be a meaner motive than this I am speaking of, in forming a judgment on this question, — that it is "better for us" — for whom? the people of England, or the government of England? — that the United States should be severed, and that that continent should be as the continent of Europe is, in many states, and subject to all the contentions and disasters which have accompanied the history of the states of Europe. (Applause.) I should say that, if a man had a great heart within him, he would rather look forward to the day when, from that point of land which is habitable nearest to the Pole, to the shores of the great Gulf, the whole of that vast continent might become one great confederation of States,—without a great army, and without a great navy,—not mixing itself up with the entanglements of European politics,—without a custom-house inside, through the whole length and breadth of its territory,—and with freedom everywhere, equality everywhere, law everywhere, peace everywhere,—such a confederation would afford at least some hope that man is not forsaken of Heaven, and that the future of our race might be better than the past. (Loud cheers.)

It is a common observation, that our friends in America are very irritable. Well, I think it is very likely, of a considerable number of them, to be quite true. Our friends in America are involved in a great struggle. There is nothing like it before in their or in any history. No country in the world was ever more entitled, in my opinion, to the sympathy and the forbearance of all friendly nations, than are the United States at this moment. (Hear! Hear!) They have there some newspapers that are no wiser than ours. (Laughter.) They have there some papers, or one at least, which, up to the election of Mr. Lincoln, were his bitterest and most unrelenting foes, who, when the war broke out, and it was not safe to take the line of Southern support, were obliged to turn round and to support the prevalent opinion of the country. But they undertook to serve the South in another way, and that was by exaggerating every difficulty, and misstating every fact, if so doing could serve their object of creating distrust between the people of the Northern States and the people of this United Kingdom. (Hear! hear!) If the *Times* in this country has done all that it could do to poison the minds of the people of England, and to irritate the minds of the people of America, the *New York Herald*, I am sorry to say, has done, I think, all that it could, or all that it dared to do, to provoke mischief between the government in Washington and the government in London.

Now there is one thing which I must state that I think they have a solid reason to complain of; and I am very sorry to have to mention it, because it blames our present foreign minister, against whom I am not anxious to say a word, and, recollecting his speech in the House of Commons, I should be slow to conclude that he had any feeling hostile to the United States government. You recollect that during the session, — it was on the 14th of May, — a proclamation came out which acknowledged the South as a belligerent power, and proclaimed the neutrality of England. A little time before that, I forget how many days, Mr. Dallas, the late Minister from the United States, had left London for Liverpool and America. He did not wish to undertake any affairs for this government, by which he was not appointed,—I mean that of President Lincoln,—and he left what had to be done to his successor, who was on his way, and whose arrival was daily expected. Mr. Adams, the present Minister from the United States, is a man who, if he lived in England, you would say was of one of the noblest families of the country. His father and his grandfather were Presidents of the United States. His grandfather was one of the great men who achieved the independence of the United States. There is no family in that country having more claims upon what I should call the veneration and the affection of the people than the family of Mr. Adams.

Mr. Adams came to this country. He arrived in London on the night of the 13th May. On the 14th, that proclamation was issued. It was known that he was coming; but he was not consulted; the proclamation was not delayed for a day, although there was nothing pressed, and he might have been notified about it. If communications of a friendly nature had taken place with him and with the American government, they could have found no fault with this step, because it was, perhaps, inevitable, before the struggle had proceeded far, that this proclamation would be issued. But I have the best reasons for knowing that there is no single thing that has happened during the course of these events which has created more surprise, more irritation, and more distrust in the United States, with respect to this country, than the fact that that proclamation was not delayed one single day, until the Minister from America could come here, and until it could be done with his consent, or at least his concurrence, and in that friendly manner that would have avoided all the unpleasantness which has occurred. (Hear!)

Now I am obliged to say,—and I say it with the utmost pain,—that without this country doing things that were hostile to the North, and without expressing affection for slavery, and, outwardly and openly, hatred for the Union,—I say that there has not been seen that friendly and cordial neutrality which, if I had been a citizen of the United States, I should have expected; and I say further, that, if there has existed considerable irritation at that, it must be taken as a measure of the high appreciation which the people of those States place upon the opinion of the people of England. (Hear! Hear!) If I had been addressing this audience ten days ago, so far as I know, I should have said just what I have said now; and although, by an untoward event, circumstances are somewhat, even considerably, altered, yet I have thought it desirable to make this statement, with a view, so far as I am able to do it, to improve the opinion in England, and to assuage them if there be any feelings of irritation in America, so that no further difficulties may arise in the progress of this unhappy strife. (Hear! Hear!)

But there has occurred an event which was announced to us only a week ago, which is one of great importance, and it may be one of some peril. (Hear! hear!) It is asserted that what is called "international law" has been broken by the seizure of the Southern Commissioners on board an English trading steamer by a steamer of war of the United States. Now, what is maritime law? You have heard that the opinions of the law officers of the Crown are in favor of this view of the case,—that the law has been broken. I am not at all going to say that it has not. It would be imprudent in me to set my opinion on a legal question which I have only partially examined, against their opinion on the same question, which I presume they have carefully examined. But this I say, that maritime law is not to be found in an act of Parliament,—it is not in so many clauses. You know that it is difficult to find the law. I can ask the Mayor, or any magistrate around me, whether it is not very difficult to find the law, — even when you have found the act of Parliament, and found the clause. (Laughter.) But when you have no act of Parliament, and no clause, you may imagine that the case is still more difficult. (Hear! Hear!)

Now, maritime law, or international law, consists of opinions and precedents for the most part, and it is very unsettled. The opinions are the opinions of men of different countries, given at different times; and the precedents are not always like each other. The law is very unsettled, and, for the most part, I believe it to be exceedingly bad. Now, in past times, as you know from the histories you read, this country has been a fighting country; we have been belligerents, and, as belligerents, we have carried maritime law, by our own powerful hand, to a pitch that has been very oppressive to foreign, and peculiarly to neutral nations. Well, now, for the first time unhappily, — almost for the first time in our history for the last two hundred years, — we are not belligerents, but neutrals; and we are more disposed to take, perhaps, rather a different view of maritime and international law.

Now, the act which has been committed by the American steamer, in my opinion, whether it was illegal or not, was both impolitic and bad. That is my opinion. I think it may turn out, and is almost certain, that, so far as the taking of those men from that ship was concerned, it was wholly unknown to, and unauthorized by, the American government. And if the American government believe, on the opinion of their law officers, that the act is illegal, I have no doubt they will make fitting reparation; for there is no government in the world that has so strenuously insisted upon modifications of international law, and been so anxious to be guided always by the most moderate and merciful interpretation of that law.

Now, our great advisers of the *Times* newspaper have been persuading people that this is merely one of a series of acts which denote the determination of the Washington government to pick a quarrel with the people of England. Did you ever know anybody who was not very near dead drunk, who, having as much upon his hands as he could manage, would offer to fight anybody about him? (Prolonged laughter and cheering.) Do you believe that the United States government, presided over by President Lincoln, so constitutional in all his acts, so moderate as he has been, — representing at this moment that great party in the United States, happily now in the ascendency, which has always been especially in favor of peace, and especially friendly to England, — do you believe that that government, having upon its hands now an insurrection of the most formidable character in the South, would invite the armies and the fleets of England to combine with that insurrection, and, it might be, to render it impossible that the Union should ever again be restored? (Loud cheers.) I say, that single statement, whether it came from a public writer or a public speaker, is enough to stamp him forever with the character of being an insidious enemy of both countries. (Cheers.)

Well, now, what have we seen during the last week? People have not been, I am told,—I have not seen much of it,—quite as calm as sensible men should be. Here is a question of law. I will undertake to say, that when you have from the United States government—if they think the act legal—a statement of their view of the case, they will show you that, fifty or sixty years ago, during the wars of that time, there were scores of cases that were at least as bad as this, and some infinitely worse. And if it were not so late to-night, and I am not anxious now to go into the question further, I could easily place before you cases of wonderful outrage committed by us when we were at war, and for many of which, I am afraid, little or no reparation was offered. But let us bear this in mind, that during this struggle incidents and accidents will happen. Bear in mind the advice of Lord Stanley, so opportune and so judicious. Do not let your newspapers, or your public speakers, or any man, take you off your guard, and bring you into that frame of mind under which your government, if it desires war, may be driven to engage in it; for one may be as fatal and as evil as the other.

What can be now more monstrous than that we, as we call ourselves to some extent, an educated, a moral, and a Christian nation,—at a moment when an accident of this kind occurs, before we have made a representation to the American government, before we have heard a word from there in reply,—should be all up in arms, every sword leaping from its scabbard, and every man looking about for his pistols and his blunderbusses? (Cheers.) I think the conduct pursued — and I have no doubt it is pursued by a certain class in America just the same — is much more the conduct of savages, than of Christian and civilized men. No, let us be calm. (Hear! Hear!) You recollect how we were dragged into the Russian war, — "drifted" into it? (Cheers.) You know that I, at least, have not upon my head any of the guilt of that fearful war. (Hear! Hear!) You know that it cost one hundred millions of money to this country; that it cost at least the lives of forty thousand Englishmen; that it disturbed your trade; that it nearly doubled the armies of Europe; that it placed the relations of Europe on a much less peaceful footing than before; and that it did not effect one single thing of all those that it was promised to effect. (Cheers.)

I recollect speaking on this subject, within the last two years, to a man whose name I have already mentioned, Sir James Graham, in the House of Commons. He was a minister at the time of that war. He was reminding me of a severe onslaught which I had made upon him and Lord Palmerston for attending a dinner of the Reform Club, when Sir Charles Napier was appointed to the command of the Baltic fleet; and he remarked, "What a severe thrashing" — (laughter) — I had given them in the House of Commons! I said, "Sir James, tell me candidly, did you not deserve it?" He said, "Well, you were entirely right about that war; we were entirely wrong, and we never should have gone into it." (Loud cheers.) And this is exactly what everybody will say, if you go into a war about this business, when it is over. When your sailors and soldiers, so many of them as may be slaughtered, are gone to their last account; when your taxes are increased, your business permanently — it may be — injured; and when embittered feelings for generations have been created between America and England, — then your statesmen will tell you that "we ought not to have gone into the war." (Cheers.)

But they will very likely say, as many of them tell me, "What could we do in the frenzy of the public mind?" Let them not add to the frenzy, — (Hear! Hear!) — and let us be careful that nobody drives us into that frenzy. Remembering the past, remembering at this moment the perils of a friendly people, and seeing the difficulties by which they are surrounded, let us, I entreat of you, see if there be any real moderation in the people of England, and if magnanimity, so often to be found amongst individuals, is absolutely wanting in a great nation. (Great cheering.)

Now, government may discuss this matter, — they may arrange it, — they may arbitrate it. I have received here, since I came into the room, a despatch from a friend of mine in London, referring to this matter. I believe some portion of it is in the papers this evening, but I have not seen them. But he states that General Scott, whom you know by name, who has come over from America to France, being in a bad state of health, — the general lately of the American army, and a man of a reputation in that country not second hardly to that which the Duke of Wellington held during his lifetime in this country, — General Scott has written a letter on the American difficulty. He denies that the Cabinet of Washington had ordered the seizure of the Southern Commissioners, even if under a neutral flag. The question of legal right involved in the seizure, the General thinks a very narrow ground on which to force a quarrel with the United States. As to Messrs. Slidell and Mason being or not being contraband, the General answers for it, that, if Mr. Seward cannot convince Earl Russell that they bore that character, Earl Russell will be able to convince Mr. Seward that they did not. He pledges himself that, if this government cordially agree with that of the United States in establishing the immunity of neutrals from the oppressive right of search and seizure on suspicion, the Cabinet of Washington will not hesitate to purchase so great a boon to peaceful trading-vessels. (Great cheering.)

Now then, before I sit down, let me ask you what is this people, about which so many men in England at this moment are writing, and speaking, and thinking, with harshness, I think with injustice, if not with great bitterness? Two centuries ago, multitudes of the people of this country found a refuge on the North American continent, escaping from the tyranny of the Stuarts, and from the bigotry of Laud. Many noble spirits from our country made great experiments in favor of human freedom on that continent. Bancroft, the great historian of his own country, has said, in his own graphic and emphatic language, "The history of the colonization of America is the history of the crimes of Europe." (Hear! Hear!) From that time down to our own period, America has admitted the wanderers from every clime. Since 1815, a time which many here remember, and which is within my lifetime, more than three millions of persons have emigrated from the United Kingdom to the United States. During the fifteen years from 1845 or 1846 to 1859 or 1860, — a time so recent that we all remember the most trivial circumstances that have happened in that time, — during those fifteen years more than two million three hundred and twenty thousand persons left the shores of the United Kingdom as emigrants for the States of North America.

At this very moment, then, there are millions in the United States who personally, or whose immediate parents, have at one time been citizens of this country, and perhaps known to some of the oldest of those whom I have now the honor of addressing. They found a home in the Far West; they subdued the wilderness; they met with plenty there, which was not afforded them in their native country; and they became a great people. There may be persons in England who are jealous of those States. There may be men who dislike democracy, and who hate a republic; there may be even those whose sympathies warm towards the slave oligarchy of the South. But of this I am certain, that only misrepresentation the most gross or calumny the most wicked can sever the tie which unites the great mass of the people of this country with their friends and brethren beyond the Atlantic. (Loud cheers.)

Now, whether the Union will be restored or not, or the South achieve an unhonored independence or not, I know not, and I predict not. But this I think I know, — that in a few years, a very few years, the twenty millions of freemen in the North will be thirty millions, or even fifty millions, — a population equal to or exceeding that of this kingdom. (Hear! Hear!) When that time comes, I pray that it may not be said amongst them, that, in the darkest hour of their country's trials, England, the land of their fathers, looked on with icy coldness and saw unmoved the perils and calamities of their children. (Cheers.) As for me, I have but this to say: I am one in this audience, and but one in the citizenship of this country; but if all other tongues are silent, mine shall speak for that policy which gives hope to the bondsmen of the South, and which tends to generous thoughts, and generous words, and generous deeds, between the two great nations who speak the English language, and from their origin are alike entitled to the English name. (Loud cheers; during which the honorable member resumed his seat, having spoken for an hour and forty minutes.)

SPEECH AT BIRMINGHAM,

DECEMBER 18, 1862.

Mr. Bright rose, and was received with the most hearty and prolonged applause. He said:—

Gentlemen, I am afraid that there was a little excitement during a part of my honorable colleague's speech, which was hardly favorable to that impartial consideration of great questions to which he appealed. (Hear! Hear!) He began by referring to a question,—or, I might say, to two questions, for it was one great question in two parts,—which at this moment occupies the mind, and, I think, must afflict the heart of every thoughtful man in this country,—(Hear! Hear!)—the calamity which has fallen upon the county from which I come, and the strife which is astonishing the world, on the other side of the Atlantic.

I shall not enter into details with regard to that calamity, because you have had already, I believe, meetings in this town, many details have been published, contributions of a generous character have been made, and you are doing — and especially, if I am rightly informed, are your artisans doing — their duty with regard to the unfortunate condition of the population amongst which I live. (Cheers.) But this I may state in a sentence, that the greatest, probably the most prosperous, manufacturing industry that this country or the world has ever seen, has been suddenly and unexpectedly stricken down, but by a blow which has not been unforeseen or unforetold. (Hear! Hear!) Nearly five hundred thousand persons, — men, women, and children, — at this moment, are saved from the utmost extremes of famine, not a few of them from death, by the contributions which they are receiving from all parts of the country. (Cheers.) I will not attempt here an elaborate eulogy of the generosity of the givers, nor will I endeavor to paint the patience and the gratitude of those who suffer and receive; but I believe the conduct of the country, with regard to this great misfortune, is an honor to all classes and to every section of this people. (Cheers.)

Some have remarked that there is perfect order where there has been so much anxiety and suffering. I believe there is scarcely a thoughtful man in Lancashire who will not admit that one great cause of the patience and good conduct of the people, besides the fact that they knew so much is being done for them, is to be found in the extensive information they possess, and which of late years, and now more than ever, has been communicated to them through the instrumentality of an untaxed press. (Loud cheers.) Noble lords who have recently spoken, official men, and public men, have taken upon them to tell the people of Lancashire that nobody is to blame, and that in point of fact, if it had not been for a family quarrel in that dreadful Republic, everything would have gone on perfectly smoothly, and not a word could have been said against anybody. (Laughter.)

Now, if you will allow me, I should like to examine for a few minutes whether this be true. (Hear! Hear!) If you read the papers with regard to this question, you will find that, barring whatever chance there may be of our again soon receiving a supply of cotton from America, the hopes of the whole country are directed to India. Our government of India is not one of today. It is a government that has lasted as long as the government of the United States, and it has had far more insurrections and secessions, — (cheers,) — not one of which, I suppose some in this meeting must regret, has been recognized by our government or by France. (Cheers.) Our government in India has existed for a hundred years in some portion of the country where cotton is a staple produce of the land. But we have had under the name of a government what I have always described as a piratical joint-stock company, — (laughter and cheers,) — beginning with Lord Clive, and ending, as I now hope it has ended, with Lord Dalhousie. (Laughter.) And under that government I will undertake to say that it was not in nature that you could have such improvement of that country as should ever give you a fair supply of cotton. (Cheers.)

Up to the year 1814, the whole trade of India was a monopoly of the East India Company. They took everything there that went there; they brought everything back that came here; they did whatsoever they pleased in the territories under their rule. I have here an extract from a report of a member of Council in India, Mr. Richards, published in the year 1812. He reports to the Court of Directors, that the whole cotton produce of the district was taken, without leaving any portion of the avowed share of the Ryots, that is, the cultivators, at their own free disposal; and he says that they are not suffered to know what they shall get for it until after it has been far removed from their reach and from the country by exportation coastwise to Bombay; and he says further, that the Company's servants fixed the prices from ten to thirty per cent under the general market rate in the districts that were not under the Company's rule. During the three years before the Company's monopoly was abolished, in 1814, the whole cotton that we received from India, I quote from the brokers' returns from Liverpool, was only 17,000 bales; in the three years afterwards, owing, no doubt, partly to the great increase in price, we received 551,000 bales, during which same three years the United States only sent us 611,000. Thus you see that in 1817, 1818, and 1819, more than forty years ago, the quantity we received from

India was close upon, and in the year 1818 it actually exceeded, that which we received from the United States.

Well, now I come down to the year 1832, and I have then the report of another member of Council, and beg every workingman here, every man who is told that there is nobody to blame, to listen to one or two extracts from the report. Mr. Warden, member of the Council, gave evidence in 1832 that the money-tax levied on Surat cotton was 56 rupees per candy, leaving the grower only 24 rupees, or rather less than $\frac{3}{4}d.$ per pound. In 1846 there was so great a decay of the cotton-trade of Western India, that a committee was appointed in Bombay, partly of members of the Chamber of Commerce and partly of servants of the government, and they made a report in which they stated that from every candy of cotton,—a candy is 7cwt. 784lbs.,—costing 80 rupees, which is 160 shillings in Bombay, the government had taken 48 rupees as land-tax and sea-duty, leaving only 32 rupees, or less than $\frac{3}{4}$*d.* per pound, to be divided among all parties, from the Bombay seller to the Surat grower. (Cheers.)

In 1847 I was in the House of Commons, and I brought forward a proposition for a select committee to inquire into this whole question; for in that year Lancashire was on the verge of the calamity that has now overtaken it; cotton was very scarce, for hundreds of the mills were working short time, and many were closed altogether. That committee reported that, in all the districts of Bombay and Madras where cotton was cultivated, and generally over those agricultural regions, the people were in a condition of the most abject and degraded pauperism; and I will ask you whether it is possible for a people in that condition to produce anything great, or anything good, or anything constant, which the world requires? (No! No!)

It is not to be wondered at that the quality

of the cotton should be bad, — so bad that it is illustrated by an anecdote which a very excellent man of the Methodist body told me the other day. He said that at a prayer-meeting, not more than a dozen miles from where I live, one of the ministers was deep in supplication to the Supreme; he detailed, no doubt, a great many things which he thought they were in want of, and amongst the rest, a supply of cotton for the famishing people in that district. When he prayed for cotton, some man with a keen sense of what he had suffered, in response, exclaimed, "O Lord! but not Surat." (Laughter.)

Now, my argument is this, and my assertion is this, that the growth of cotton in India, — the growth of an article which was native and common in India before America was discovered by Europeans, — that the growth of that article has been systematically injured, strangled, and destroyed by the stupid and wicked policy of the Indian government. (Cheers.)

I saw, the other day, a letter from a gentleman as well acquainted with Indian affairs, perhaps, as any man in India, — a letter written to a member of the Madras Government, — in which he stated his firm opinion that, if it had not been for the Bombay Committee in 1846, and for my committee in 1848, there would not have been any cotton sent from India at this moment to be worked up in Lancashire. Now, in 1846, the quantity of cotton coming from India had fallen to 94,000 bales. How has it increased since then? In 1859 it had reached 509,000 bales; in 1860, 562,000 bales; and last year, owing to the extraordinary high price, it had reached 986,000 bales, and I suppose this year will be about the same as last year.

I think, in justification of myself and of some of those with whom I have acted, I am entitled to ask your time for a few moments, to show you what has been not so much done as attempted to be done to improve this state of things; and what has been the systematic opposition that we have had to contend with. In the year 1847, I moved for that committee, in a speech from which I shall read one short extract. I said that "We ought not to forget that the whole of the cotton grown in America is produced by slave labor, and this, I think, all will admit, — that, no matter as to the period in which slavery may have existed, abolished it will ultimately be, either by peaceable means or by violent means. Whether it comes to an end by peaceable means or otherwise, there will in all probability be an interruption to the production of cotton, and the calamity which must in consequence fall upon a part of the American Union will be felt throughout the manufacturing districts of this country." (Cheers.)

The committee was not refused; — governments do not always refuse committees; they don't much fear them on matters of this kind; they put as many men on as the mover of the committee does, and sometimes more, and they often consider a committee, as my honorable colleague will tell you, rather a convenient way of burying an unpleasant question, at least for another session. The committee sat during the session of 1848, and it made a report from which I shall quote, not an extract, but the sense of an extract. The evidence was very extensive, very complete, and entirely condemnatory of the whole system of the Indian government with regard to the land and agricultural produce, and one might have hoped that something would have arisen from it, and probably something has arisen from it, but so slowly that you have no fruit, — nothing on which you can calculate, even up to this hour.

Well, in 1850, as nothing more was done, I thought it time to take another step, and I gave notice of a motion for the appointment of a Royal Commission to go to India for the express purpose of ascertaining the truth of this matter. I moved, "That a Royal Commission proceed to India to inquire into the obstacles which prevent the increased growth of cotton in India, and to report upon any circumstance which may injuriously affect the economical and industrial condition of the native population, being cultivators of the soil, within the Presidencies of Madras and Bombay."

Now I shall read you one extract from my speech on that occasion, which refers to this question of peril in America. I said, "But there is another point, that, whilst the production of cotton in the United States results from slave labor, whether we approve of any particular mode of abolishing slavery in any country or not, we are all convinced that it will be impossible in any country, and most of all in America, to keep between two and three millions of the population permanently in a state of bondage. By whatever means that system is to be abolished, whether by insurrection, — which I would deplore, — or by some great measure of justice from the government, — one thing is certain, that the production of cotton must be interfered with for a considerable time after such an event has taken place; and it may happen that the greatest measure of freedom that has ever been conceded may be a measure the consequence of which will inflict mischief upon the greatest industrial pursuit that engages the labor of the operative population of this country." (Cheers.)

Now, it was not likely the government could pay much attention to this, for at that precise moment the Foreign Office — then presided over by Lord Palmerston — was engaged with an English fleet in the waters of Greece, in collecting a bad debt, — (a laugh,) — for one Don Pacifico, a Jew who made a fraudulent demand on the Greek government for injuries said to have been committed upon him in Greece. Notwithstanding this, I called upon Lord

John Russell, who was then the Prime Minister and asked him whether he would grant the commission I was going to move for. I will say this for him, he appeared to agree with me, that it was a reasonable thing. I believe he saw the peril, and that my proposition was a proper one, but he said he wished he could communicate with Lord Dalhousie. But it was in the month of June, and he could not do that, and hear from him again before the close of the session. He told me that Sir John Hobhouse, then President of the India Board, was very much against it; and I answered, "Doubtless he is, because he speaks as the mouthpiece of the East India Company, against whom I am bringing this inquiry."

Well, my proposition came before the House, and, as some of you may recollect, it was opposed by the President of the India Board, and the Commission was consequently not granted. I had seen Sir Robert Peel,—this was only ten days before his death,—I had seen Sir Robert Peel, acquainted as he was with Lancashire interests, and had endeavored to enlist him in my support. He cordially and entirely approved of my motion, and he remained in the House during the whole of the time I was speaking; but when Sir John Hobhouse rose to resist the motion, and he found the government would not consent to it, he then left his seat, and left the House. The night after, or two nights after, he met me in the lobby; and he said he thought it was but right he should explain why he left the House after the conversation he had held with me on this question before. He said he had hoped the government would agree to the motion, but when he found they would not, his position was so delicate with regard to them and his own old party, that he was most anxious that nothing should induce him, unless under the pressure of some great extremity, to appear even to oppose them on any matter before the House. Therefore, from a very delicate sense of honor he did not say what I am sure he would have been glad to have said, and the proposition did not receive from him that help which, if it had received it, would have surmounted all obstacles.

To show the sort of men who are made ministers, — (laughter,) — Sir John Hobhouse had on these occasions always a speech of the same sort. He said this: "With respect to the peculiar urgency of the time, he could not say the honorable gentleman had made out his case; for he found that the importation of cotton from all countries showed an immense increase during the last three years." Why, we know that the importation of cotton has shown an "immense increase" almost every three years for the last fifty years. (Hear! Hear! and a laugh.) But it was because that increase was entirely, or nearly so, from one source, and that source one of extreme peril, that I asked for the inquiry for which I moved. (Cheers.) He said he had a letter — and he shook it at me in his hand — from the Secretary of the Commercial Association of Manchester, in which the directors of that body declared by special resolution that my proposition was not necessary, that an inquiry might do harm, and that they were abundantly satisfied with everything that these Lords of Leadenhall Street were doing. He said, "Such was the letter of the Secretary of the Association, and it was a complete answer to the honorable gentleman who had brought forward this motion."

At this moment one of these gentlemen to whom I have referred, then President of the Board of Control, Governor of India, author, as he told a committee on which I sat, of the Affghan war, is now decorated with a Norman title, — for our masters even after a lapse of eight hundred years ape the Norman style, — sits in the House of Peers, and legislates for you, having neglected in regard to India every great duty which appertained to his high office, — (tremendous applause,) — and to show that it is not only cabinets and monarchs who thus distribute honors and rewards, the President of that Commercial Association through whose instigation that letter was written is now one of the representatives of Manchester, the great centre of that manufacture whose very foundation is now crumbling into ruin. (Renewed cheering.)

But I was not, although discouraged, baffled. I went down to the Chamber of Commerce in Manchester, and along with Mr. Bazley, then the President of the Chamber, I believe, and Mr. Ashworth, who is now the President of that Chamber, and many others, we determined to have a Commission of Inquiry of our own. We raised a subscription of more than £2,000; we selected a gentleman, — Mr. Alexander Mackay, the author of one of the very best books ever written by an Englishman upon America, "The Western World,"—and we invited him to become our Commissioner, and, unfortunately for him, he accepted the office. He went to India, he made many inquiries, he wrote many interesting reports, but, like many others who go to India, his health declined; he returned from Bombay, but he did not live to reach home.

We were greatly disappointed at this on public grounds, besides our regret for the loss of one of so much private worth. Some of us, Mr. Bazley particularly, undertook the charge of publishing these reports, and a friend of Mr. Mackay's, now no longer living, undertook the editorship of them, and they were published in a volume called "Western India"; and that volume received such circulation as a work of that nature is likely to have. (Hear! Hear!)

Well, now, in 1853 there came the proposition for the renewal of the East India Company's charter. I opposed that to the utmost of my power in the House of Commons, — (loud cheers,) — and some of you will recollect I came down here with Mr. Danby Seymour, the member for Poole, a gentleman well acquainted with Indian affairs, and attended a meeting in this very hall, to denounce the policy of conferring the government of that great country for another twenty years upon a company which had so entirely neglected every duty belonging to it except one, — the duty of collecting the taxes. (Much laughter and cheers.) In 1854, Colonel Cotton — now Sir Arthur Cotton, one of the most distinguished engineers in India — came down to Manchester. We had a meeting at the Town Hall, and he gave an address on the subject of opening the Godavery River, in order that it might form a mode of transit, cheap and expeditious, from the cotton districts to the north of that river; and it was proposed to form a joint stock company to do it, but unfortunately the Russian war came on and disturbed all commercial projects, and made it impossible to raise money for any — as some might call it — speculative purpose, like that of opening an Indian river.

Well, in 1857 there came the mutiny. What did our rulers do then? Sir Charles Wood, in 1853, had made a speech five hours long, most of it bolstering up the government of the East India Company. In 1858, — at the opening of the session in 1858, I think, — the government brought in a bill to abolish that Company, and to establish a new form of government for India. That was exactly what we asked them to do in 1853; but, as in everything else, nothing is done until there comes an overwhelming calamity, when the most obtuse and perverse is driven from his position. (Applause.) In 1858 that bill passed, under the auspices of Lord Stanley. It was not a bill such as I think Lord Stanley approved when he was not a minister; it was not a bill such as I believe he would have brought in if he had had power in the House and the Cabinet to have brought in a better bill. It abolished the East India Company, established a new Council, and left things to a great extent much in the same state as they were.

During the discussion of that bill, I made a speech on Indian affairs, which I believe goes to the root of the matter. I protested then as now against any notion of governing one hundred and fifty millions of people — twenty different nations, with twenty different languages — from a little coterie of rulers in the city of Calcutta. (Cheers.) I proposed that the country should be divided into four or five separate, and, as regards each other, independent presidencies of equal rank, with a governor and council in each, and each government corresponding with, and dependent upon, and responsible to, a Secretary of State in this country.

(Loud cries of "Hear! Hear!" and cheers.) I am of opinion that if such a government were established, one in each Presidency, and if there was a first-class engineer, with an efficient staff, whose business should be to determine what public works should be carried on, some by the government and some by private companies, — I believe that ten years of such judicious labors would work an entire revolution in the condition of India; and if it had been done when I first began to move in this question, I have not the smallest doubt we might have had at this moment any quantity of cotton whatever that the mills of Lancashire require. (Great cheering.)

Well, after this, I am afraid some of my friends may think, and my opponents will say, that it is very egotistical in me to have entered into these details. (Cries of "No! No!") But I think, after this recapitulation, I am at liberty to say I am guiltless of that calamity which has fallen upon us.

(Tremendous applause.) And I may mention that some friends of mine — Mr. John Dickinson, now Chairman of the India Reform Association, Mr. Bazley, one of the members for Manchester, Mr. Ashworth, the President of the Chamber of Commerce of Manchester, and Mr. John Benjamin Smith, the member for Stockport — present themselves at this moment to my eyes as those who have been largely instrumental in calling the attention of Parliament and of the country to this great question of the reform of our government of India. (Cheers.)

But I have been asked twenty, fifty times during the last twelve months, "Why don't you come out and say something? Why can't you tell us something in this time of our great need?" Well, I reply, "I told you something when telling was of use; all I can say now is this, or nearly all, that a hundred years of crime against the negro in America, and a hundred years of crime against the docile natives of our Indian empire, are not to be washed away by the penitence and the suffering of an hour." (Great cheering.)

But what is our position? for you who are subscribing your money here have a right to know. I believe the quantity of cotton in the United States is at this moment much less than many people here believe, and that it is in no condition to be forwarded and exported. And I suspect that it is far more probable than otherwise, notwithstanding some of the, I should say, strange theories of my honorable colleague, that there never will again be in America a crop of cotton grown by slave labor. (Great cheering.) You will understand,— I hope so at least,—that I am not undertaking the office of prophet, I am not predicting; I know that everything which is not absolutely impossible may happen, and therefore things may happen wholly different to the course which appears to me likely. But I say, taking the facts as they are before us, — with that most limited vision which is given to mortals, — the high probability is that there will never be another crop considerable or of avail in our manufactories from slave labor in the United States. (Renewed cheers.)

We read the American papers, or the quotations from them in our own papers, but I believe we can form no adequate conception of the disorganization and chaos that now prevail throughout a great portion of the Southern States; it is natural to a state of war under the circumstances of society in that region. But then we may be asked, What are our sources of supply, putting aside India? There is the colony of Queensland, where enthusiastic persons tell you cotton can be grown worth 3*s.* a pound. True enough; but when labor is probably worth 10*s.* a day, I am not sure you are likely to get any large supply of that material we so much want, at a rate so cheap that we shall be likely to use it. (Hear!

Hear!) Africa is pointed to by a very zealous friend of mine; but Africa is a land of savages mostly, and with its climate so much against European constitutions, I should not encourage the hope that any great relief at any early period can be had from that continent. (Hear! Hear!) Egypt will send us 30,000 or 40,000 more bales than last year; in all probability Syria and Brazil, with these high prices, will increase their production to some considerable extent; but I hold that there is no country at present from which you can derive any very large supply, except you can get it from your own dependencies in India. (Cheers.) Now if there be no more cotton to be grown for two, or three, or four years in America, for our supply, we shall require, considering the smallness of the bales and the loss in working up the cotton, — we shall require nearly 6,000,000 of additional bales to be supplied from some source.

Now I want to put to you one question.

It has taken the United States twenty years, from 1840 up to 1860, to increase their growth of cotton from 2,000,000 of bales to 4,000,000. How long will it take any other country, with comparatively little capital, with a thousand disadvantages which America did not suffer from, — how long will it take any other country, or all other countries, to give us 5,000,000 or 6,000,000 additional bales of cotton? (Hear! Hear!) There is one stimulus, — the only one that I know of; and although I have not recommended it to the government, and I know not precisely what sacrifice it would entail, yet I shall mention it, and I do it on the authority of a gentleman to whom I have before referred, who is thoroughly acquainted with Indian agriculture, and who, himself and his father, have been land-owners and cultivators in India for sixty years. He says there is only one mode by which you can rapidly stimulate the growth of cotton in India, except that stimulus coming from the high prices for the time being, — he says that, if the government would make a public declaration that for five years they would exempt from land tax all land which during that time shall grow cotton, there would be the most extraordinary increase in the growth of that article which has ever been seen in regard to any branch of agriculture in the world. (Much applause.)

I don't know how far that would act, but I believe the stimulus would be enormous, — the loss to the government in revenue would be something, but the deliverance to the industry of Lancashire, if it succeeded, as my friend thinks, would, of course, be speedy, and perhaps complete. Short of this, I look upon the restoration of the prosperity of Lancashire as distant, — most remote. I believe this misfortune will entail ruin upon the whole working population, and that it will gradually engulf the smaller traders and those possessing the least capital. I don't say it will, because, as I have said, what is not impossible may happen,—but it may for years make the whole factory property of Lancashire almost entirely worthless. (Loud cries of "Hear! Hear!") Well, this is a very dismal look-out for a great many persons in this country; but it comes, as I have said,—it comes from that utter neglect of our opportunities and our duties which has distinguished the government of India. (Applause.)

Now, sir, before I sit down I shall ask you to listen to me for a few moments on the other branch of this great question, which refers to that sad tragedy which is passing before our eyes in the United States of America. (Hear! Hear!) I shall not, in consequence of anything you have heard from my honorable friend, conceal from you any of the opinions which I hold, and which I proposed to lay before you if he had not spoken. (Hear! Hear!) Having given to him, notwithstanding some diversity of opinion, a fair and candid hearing, I presume that I shall receive the same favor from those who may differ from me. (Hear! Hear!) If I had known that my honorable friend was going to make an elaborate speech on this occasion, one of two things I should have done. I should either have prepared myself entirely to answer him, or I should have decided not to attend a meeting where there could by any possibility of chance have been anything like discord between so many — his friends and my friends — in this room.

Since I have been member for Birmingham, Mr. Scholefield has treated me with the kindness of a brother. (Applause.) Nothing could possibly be more generous and more disinterested in every way than his conduct towards me during these several years, and therefore I would much rather — far rather — that I lost any mere opportunity like this of speaking on this question, than I would have come here and appeared to be at variance with him. But I am happy to say that this great question does not depend upon the opinion of any man in Birmingham, or in England, or anywhere else. (Cheers.) And therefore I could — anxious always, unless imperative duty requires to avoid even a semblance of difference — I could with a clear conscience have abstained from coming to and speaking at this meeting.

But I observe that my honorable friend endeavored to avoid committing himself to what is called a sympathy with the South. He takes a political view of this great question, — is disposed to deal with the matter as he would have dealt with the case of a colony of Spain or Portugal revolting in South America, or Greece revolting from Turkey. I should like to state here what I once stated to an eminent American. He asked me if I could give him an idea of the course of public opinion in this country from the moment we heard of the secession of the Cotton States; and I endeavored to trace it in this way, — and I ask you to say whether it is a fair and full description.

I said, — and my honorable friend has admitted that, — that when the revolt or secession was first announced, people here were generally against the South. (Hear! Hear!) Nobody thought then that the South had any cause for breaking up the integrity of that great nation. Their opinion was, and what people said, according to their different politics, in this country was, "They have a government which is mild, and not in any degree oppressive; they have not what some people love very much, and what some people dislike, — they have not a costly monarchy, and an aristocracy, creating and living on patronage. They have not an expensive foreign policy; a great army; a great navy; and they have no suffering millions to be discontented and endeavoring to overthrow their government; — all of which things have been said against governments in this country and in Europe a hundred times within our own hearing," — and therefore, they said, "Why should these men revolt?"

But for a moment the Washington government appeared paralyzed. It had no army and navy; everybody was traitor to it. It was paralyzed and apparently helpless; and in the hour when the government was transferred from President Buchanan to President Lincoln, many people — such was the unprepared state of the North, such was the apparent paralysis of everything there — thought there would be no war; and men shook hands with each other pleasantly, and congratulated themselves that the disaster of a great strife, and the mischief to our own trade, might be avoided. That was the opinion at that moment, so far as I can recollect, and could gather at the time, with my opportunities of gathering such opinion. They thought the North would acquiesce in the rending of the Republic, and that there would be no war.

Well, but there was another reason. They were told by certain public writers in this country that the contest was entirely hopeless, as they have been told lately by the Chancellor of the Exchequer. (Laughter.) I am very happy that, though the Chancellor of the Exchequer is able to decide to a penny what shall be the amount of taxes to meet public expenditure in England, he cannot decide what shall be the fate of a whole continent. (Hear! Hear!) It was said that the contest was hopeless, and why should the North continue a contest at so much loss of blood and treasure, and so great a loss to the commerce of the whole world. If a man thought — if a man believed in his heart that the contest was absolutely hopeless, — no man in this country had probably any right to form a positive opinion one way or the other, — but if he had formed that opinion, he might think, "Well, the North can never be successful; it would be much better that they should not carry on the war at all; and therefore I am rather glad that the South should have success, for by that the war will be the sooner put an end to." I think that was a feeling that was abroad. (Hear! Hear!)

Now I am of opinion that, if we judge a foreign nation in the circumstances in which we find America, we ought to apply it to our own principles. My honorable friend has referred, I think, to the question of the Trent. I was not here last year, but I heard of a meeting,—I read in the papers of a meeting held in reference to that affair in this very hall, and that there was a great diversity of opinion. But the majority were supposed to indorse the policy of the government in making a great demonstration of force. And I think I read that at least one minister of religion took that view from this platform. (Hear! Hear!) I am not complaining of it. But I say that if you thought when the American captain, even if he had acted under the commands of his government, which he had not, had taken two men most injurious and hostile to his country from the deck of an English ship, — if you thought that on that ground you were justified in going to war with the Republic of North America, then I say you ought not to be very nice in judging what America should do in circumstances much more onerous than those in which you were placed. (Cheers.)

Now, take as an illustration the Rock of Gibraltar. Many of you have been there, I dare say. I have; and among the things that interested me were the monkeys on the top of it, — (laughter,) — and a good many people at the bottom, who were living on English taxes. (Renewed laughter.) Well, the Rock of Gibraltar was taken and retained by this country when we were not at war with Spain, and it was retained contrary to every moral and honorable code. (A voice, "No! No!") No doubt the gentleman below is much better acquainted with the history of it than I am, — (loud laughter,) — but I may suggest to him that very likely we have read two different histories. (Renewed laughter.) But I will let this pass, and I will assume that it came into the possession of England in the most honorable way, which is, I suppose, by regular and acknowledged national warfare.

Suppose, at this moment, you heard, or the English government heard, that Spain was equipping expeditions, by land and sea, for the purpose of retaking that fortress and rock. Now, although it is not of the slightest advantage to any Englishman living, excepting to those who have pensions and occupations upon it; although every government knows it, and although more than one government has been anxious to give it up, and I hope this government will send my friend, Mr. Cobden, to Madrid, with an offer that Gibraltar shall be ceded to Spain, as being of no use to this country, and only embittering, as statesmen have admitted, the relations between Spain and England, (if he were to go to Madrid with an offer of the Rock of Gibraltar, I believe he might have a commercial treaty with Spain, that would admit every English manufacture and every article of English produce into that country at a duty of not more than ten per cent), — (Applause,) — I say, don't you think that, if you heard Spain was about to retake that useless rock, mustering her legions and her fleets, the English government would combine all the power of this country to resist it? (Applause.)

If that be so, then I think — seeing that there was a fair election two years ago, and that President Lincoln was fairly and honestly elected — that when the Southern leaders met at Montgomery in Alabama, on the 6th of March, and authorized the raising of a hundred thousand men, and when, on the 15th of April, they attacked Fort Sumter, — not a fort of South Carolina, but a fort of the Union, — then, upon all the principles that Englishmen and English governments have ever acted upon, President Lincoln was justified in calling out seventy-five thousand men, — which was his first call, — for the purpose of maintaining the integrity of that nation, which was the main purpose of the oath which he had taken at his election. (Loud cheers.)

Now I shall not go into a long argument upon this question, for the reason that a year ago I said what I thought it necessary to say upon it, and because I believe the question is in the hand, not of my honorable friend, nor in that of Lord Palmerston, nor in that even of President Lincoln, but it is in the hand of the Supreme Ruler, who is bringing about one of those great transactions in history which men often will not regard when it is passing before them, but which they look back upon with awe and astonishment some years after they are past. (Loud cheers.) So I shall content myself with asking one or two questions. I shall not discuss the question whether the North is making war for the Constitution, or making war for the abolition of slavery.

If you come to a matter of sympathy with the South, or recognition of the South, or mediation or intervention for the benefit of the South, you should consider what are the ends of the South. (Hear! Hear!) Surely the United States government is a government at amity with this country. Its Minister is in London,—a man honorable by family, as you know, in America, his father and his grandfather having held the office of President of the Republic. You have your own Minister just returned to Washington. Is this hypocrisy? Are you, because you can cavil at certain things which the North, the United States government, has done, or has not done,—are you eagerly to throw the influence of your opinion into a movement which is to dismember the great Republic? ("No! No!")

Is there a man here that doubts for a moment that the object of the war on the part of the South, — they began the war, — (Applause,) — that the object of the war on the part of the South is to maintain the bondage of four millions of human beings? (Cries of "No! No!" overwhelmed by tremendous cheering.) That is only a small part of it. The further object is to perpetuate forever the bondage of all the posterity of those four millions of slaves. (Prolonged cheering, mingled with some dissentient voices.) You will hear that I am not in a condition to contest vigorously anything that may be opposed, for I am suffering, as nearly everybody is, from the state of the weather, and a hoarseness that somewhat hinders me in speaking. I could quote their own documents till twelve o'clock in proof of what I say; and if I found a man who denied, upon the evidence that had been offered, I would not offend him, or trouble myself by trying further to convince him. (Hear! Hear!)

The object is, that a handful of white men on that continent shall lord it over countless millions of blacks, made black by the very hand that made us white. (Prolonged applause.) The object is, that they should have the power to breed negroes, to work negroes, to lash negroes, to chain negroes, to buy and sell negroes, to deny them the commonest ties of family, or to break their hearts by rending them at their pleasure, to close their mental eye to but a glimpse of that knowledge which separates us from the brute, — for in their laws it is criminal and penal to teach the negro to read, — to seal from their hearts the book of our religion, and to make chattels and things of men and women and children. (Loud and prolonged cheers.)

Now I want to ask whether this is to be the foundation, as it is proposed, of a new slave empire, and whether it is intended that on this audacious and infernal basis England's new ally is to be built up. (Renewed cheers, and cries of "No.") It has been said that Greece was recognized, and that other countries had been recognized. Why Greece was not recognized till after they had fought Turkey for six years,—(Hear! Hear!)—and the republics of South America, some of them, till they had fought the mother country for a score of years. France did not recognize the United States of America till some, I think, six years, five certainly, after the beginning of the War of Independence, and even then it was received as a declaration of war by the English government. (Applause.) I want to know who they are who speak eagerly in favor of England becoming the ally and friend of this great conspiracy against human nature. (Loud cheers.)

Now I should have no kind of objection to recognize a country because it was a country that held slaves,—to recognize the United States, or to be in amity with it. The question of slavery there, and in Cuba, and in Brazil, is, as far as respects the present generation, an accident, and it would be monstrous that we should object to trade with, and have political relations with a country, merely because it happened to have within its borders the institution of slavery, hateful as that institution is. But in this case it is a new state intending to set itself up on the sole basis of slavery. (Cries of "No!" "No!" which were drowned in cheers.) Slavery is blasphemously set up to be its chief corner-stone.

I have heard that there are ministers of state who are in favor of the South; that there are members of the aristocracy who are terrified at the shadow of the Great Republic; that there are rich men on our commercial exchanges, depraved, it may be, with their riches, and thriving unwholesomely within the atmosphere of a privileged class; that there are conductors of the public press who would barter the rights of millions of their fellow-creatures that they might bask in the smiles of the great. (Mingled approbation and disapprobation.)

But I know that there are ministers of state who do not wish that this insurrection should break up the American nation; that there are members of our aristocracy who are not afraid of the shadow of the Republic; that there are rich men, many, who are not depraved by their riches; and that there are public writers of eminence and honor, who will not barter human rights for the patronage of the great. But most of all, and before all, I believe,—I am sure it is true in Lancashire, where the workingmen have seen themselves coming down from prosperity to ruin, from independence to a subsistence on charity,—I say that I believe that the unenfranchised but not hopeless millions of this country will never sympathize with a revolt which is intended to destroy the liberty of a continent, and to build on its ruins a mighty fabric of human bondage. (Prolonged cheers.)

When I speak to gentlemen in private upon this matter, and hear their own candid opinion, — I mean those who differ from me on this matter, — they generally end by saying that the Republic is too great and too powerful, and that it is better for us — not "us," meaning you, but the governing classes, and the governing policy of England — that it should be broken up. But we will suppose that we are in New York or Boston, and are discussing England; and if any one there were to say that England has grown too big, — not in the thirty-one millions that it has in its own island, but in the one hundred and fifty millions it has in Asia, and nobody knows how many millions in every other part of the globe, — and surely an American might fairly say that he has not covered the ocean with fleets of force, or left the bones of his citizens to blanch on a hundred European battle-fields, — he could say, and a thousand times more fairly say, that England was great and powerful, and that it would be perilous for the world that she should be so great. (Applause.)

But bear in mind that every declaration of this kind, whether from an Englishman who professes to be strictly English, or from an American strictly American, or from a Frenchman strictly French, whether he talks in a proud and arrogant strain, and says that Britannia rules the waves, or whether, as an American, he speaks of "manifest destiny," and of all creation adoring the "stars and stripes," or a Frenchman who thinks that the eagles of that nation, having once overrun Europe, may possibly have a right to repeat the experiment, — I say all these ideas and all that language are to be condemned. It is not truly patriotic; it is not rational; it is not moral. Then, I say, if any man wishes that Republic to be severed on that ground, in my opinion he is only doing what tends to keep alive jealousies which in his hand will never die; and if they do not die, for anything I see, wars must be eternal.

But then I shall be told that the North do not like us at all. In fact, we have heard it to-night. It is not at all necessary that they should like us. (Laughter.) If an American be in this room to-night, will he think he likes my honorable friend? But if the North does not like England, does anybody believe the South does? It does not appear to me to be a question of liking or disliking. Everybody knows that when the South was in power, — and it has been in power for the last fifty years, — everybody knows that hostility to this country, wherever it existed in America, was cherished and stimulated to the utmost degree by some of those very men who are now leaders of this very insurrection.

My honorable friend read a passage about the Alabama. I undertake to say that he is not acquainted with the facts about the Alabama. (Laughter.) That he will admit,

I think. (Renewed laughter.) The government of this country have admitted that the building of the Alabama, and her sailing from the Mersey, was a violation of international law. In America they say, and they say here, that the Alabama is a ship of war; that she was built in the Mersey; that she was built, it is said, and I have reason to believe it, by a member of the British Parliament; that she is furnished with guns of English manufacture and produce; that she is sailed almost entirely by Englishmen; and that these facts were represented, as I know they were represented, to the collector of customs in Liverpool, who pooh-poohed them, and said there was nothing in them. He was requested to send the facts up to London to the Customs' authorities, and their solicitor, not a very wise man, but probably in favor of breaking up the Republic, did not think them of much consequence; but afterwards the opinion of an eminent counsel, Mr. Collier, the member for Plymouth, was taken, and he stated distinctly that what was being done in Liverpool was a direct infringement of the Foreign Enlistment Act, and that the Customs' authorities of Liverpool would be responsible for anything that happened in consequence.

When this opinion was taken to the Foreign Office the Foreign Office was a little astonished and a little troubled; and after they had consulted their own law officers, whose opinions agreed with that of Mr. Collier, they did what government officers generally do, and as promptly, — a telegraphic message went down to Liverpool to order that this vessel should be arrested, and she happened to sail an hour or two before the message arrived. (Laughter.) She has never been into a Confederate port, — they have not got any ports; she hoists the English flag when she wants to come alongside a ship; she sets a ship on fire in the night, and when, seeing fire, another ship bears down to lend help, she seizes it, and pillages and burns it. I think that, if we were citizens of New York, it would require a little more calmness than is shown in this country to look at all this as if it was a matter with which we had no concern. And therefore I do not so much blame the words that have been said in America in reference to that question. (Hear! Hear!)

But they do not know in America so much as we know,—the whole truth about public opinion here. There are ministers in our Cabinet as resolved to be no traitors to freedom, on this question, as I am; and there are members of the English aristocracy, and in the very highest rank as I know for a certainty, who hold the same opinion. (Applause.) They do not know in America—at least there has been no indication of it until the advices that have come to hand within the last two days—what is the opinion of the great body of the working classes in England. There has been every effort that money and malice could use to stimulate in Lancashire, amongst the suffering population, an expression of opinion in favor of the Slave States. They have not been able to get it. (Loud cheers.) And I honor that population for their fidelity to principles and to freedom, and I say that the course they have taken ought to atone in the minds of the people of the United States for miles of leading articles, written by the London press, — by men who would barter every human right, — that they might serve the party with which they are associated.

But now I shall ask you one other question before I sit down, — How comes it that on the Continent there is not a liberal newspaper, nor a liberal politician, that durst say, or ever thought of saying, a word in favor of this portentous and monstrous shape which now asks to be received into the family of nations? Take the great Italian minister, Count Cavour. You read some time ago in the papers part of a despatch which he wrote on the question of America, — he had no difficulty in deciding. Ask Garibaldi. (Cheers.) Is there in Europe a more disinterested and generous friend of freedom than Garibaldi? (Cheers, and "No! No!") Ask that illustrious Hungarian, to whose marvellous eloquence you once listened in this hall. Will he tell you that slavery had nothing to do with it, and that the slaveholders of the South would liberate the negroes sooner than the North through the instrumentality of the war? (Cheers.) Ask Victor Hugo, the poet of freedom, — the exponent, may I not call him, of the yearnings of all mankind for a better time. Ask any man in Europe who opens his lips for freedom, — who dips his pen in ink that he may indite a sentence for freedom, — whoever has a sympathy for freedom warm in his own heart, — ask him, — he will have no difficulty in telling you on which side your sympathies should lie. (Cheers.)

Only a few days ago a German merchant in Manchester was speaking to a friend of mine, and said he had recently travelled all through Germany. He said, "I am so surprised, — I don't find one man in favor of the South." That is not true of Germany only, it is true of all the world except this island, famed for freedom, in which we dwell. I will tell you what is the reason. Our London press is mainly in the hands of certain ruling West End classes; it acts and writes in favor of those classes. I will tell you what they mean. One of the most eminent statesmen in this country, — one who has rendered the greatest services to the country, though, I must say, not in an official capacity, in which men very seldom confer such great advantages upon the country, — he told me twice, at an interval of several months, "I had no idea how much influence the example of that Republic was having upon opinion here, until I discovered the universal congratulation that the Republic was likely to be broken up."

But, sir, the Free States are the home of the workingman. Now, I speak to workingmen particularly at this moment. Do you know that in fifteen years two million five hundred thousand persons, men, women, and children, have left the United Kingdom to find a home in the Free States of America? That is a population equal to eight great cities of the size of Birmingham. What would you think of eight Birminghams being transplanted from this country and set down in the United States? Speaking generally, every man of these two and a half millions is in a position of much higher comfort and prosperity than he would have been if he had remained in this country. I say it is the home of the workingman; as one of her poets has recently said,

> "For her free latch-string never was drawn in
> Against the poorest child of Adam's kin."

(Great cheering.) And there, there are no

six millions of grown men — I speak of the Free States — excluded from the Constitution of their country and their electoral franchise; there, there is a free Church, — (Cheers,) — a free school, free land, a free vote, and a free career for the child of the humblest born in the land. (Renewed cheers.) My countrymen who work for your living, remember this; there will be one wild shriek of freedom to startle all mankind, if that American Republic should be overthrown. (Applause.)

Now for one moment let us lift ourselves, if we can, above the narrow circle in which we are all too apt to live, and think; let us put ourselves on an historical eminence, and judge this matter fairly. Slavery has been, as we all know, the huge, foul blot upon the fame of the American Republic; it is a hideous outrage against human right and against Divine law; but the pride, the passion of man, will not permit its peaceable extinction; the slave-owners of our colonies, if they had been strong enough, would have revolted too. I believe there was no mode short of a miracle more stupendous than any recorded in Holy Writ that could in our time, or in a century, have brought about the abolition of slavery in America, but the suicide which the South has committed and the war which it has commenced. (Cheers.)

Sir, it is a measureless calamity,—this war. I said the Russian war was a measureless calamity, and yet many of your leaders and friends told you that was a just war to maintain the integrity of Turkey, some thousands of miles off. Surely the integrity of your own country at your own doors must be worth as much as the integrity of Turkey. (Hear! Hear!) Is not this war the penalty which inexorable justice exacts from America, North and South, for the enormous guilt of cherishing that frightful iniquity of slavery for the last eighty years? I do not blame any man here who thinks the cause of the North hopeless, and the restoration of the Union impossible. It may be hopeless; the restoration may be impossible. You have the authority of the Chancellor of the Exchequer on that point. (Laughter.) The Chancellor, as a speaker, is not surpassed by any man in England; but unfortunately he made use of expressions in the North of England, — now, I suppose, nearly three months ago, — and he seems to have been engaged during the whole succeeding three months in trying to make people understand what he meant. (Laughter.) But this is obvious, — that he believes the cause of the North to be hopeless; that their enterprise cannot succeed.

Well, he is quite welcome to that opinion, and so is anybody else. I do not hold the opinion; but the facts are before us all, and, as far as we can discard passion and sympathy, we are all equally at liberty to form our own opinion. But what I do blame is this. I blame men who are eager to admit into the family of nations a state which offers itself to you as based upon a principle, I will undertake to say, more odious and more blasphemous than was ever heretofore dreamed of in Christian or Pagan, in civilized or in savage times. (Loud cheers.) The leaders of this revolt propose this monstrous thing, — that over a territory forty times as large as England the blight and curse of slavery shall be forever perpetuated.

I cannot believe, myself, in such a fate befalling that fair land, stricken as it now is with the ravages of war. (Cheering.) I cannot believe that civilization in its journey with the sun will sink into endless night to gratify the ambition of the leaders of this revolt, who seek to

> "Wade through slaughter to a throne,
> And shut the gates of mercy on mankind."

(Enthusiastic applause.) I have a far other and far brighter vision before my gaze. (Renewed cheering.) It may be but a vision, but I will cherish it. I see one vast confederation stretching from the frozen North in unbroken line to the glowing South, and from the wild billows of the Atlantic westward to the calmer waters of the Pacific main, — and I see one people, and one law, and one language, and one faith, and, over all that wide continent, the home of freedom, and a refuge for the oppressed of every race and of every clime.

(The honorable gentleman resumed his seat amid an enthusiastic burst of cheering.)

SPEECH ON SLAVERY AND SECESSION.

A PUBLIC meeting of the inhabitants of Rochdale was held in the Public Hall, Baillie Street, February 3, 1863, for the purpose of passing a resolution of thanks to the American subscribers in aid of the unemployed work-people of Lancashire. The meeting was convened by the Mayor, in accordance with a requisition signed by one hundred and seventy-six persons. The hall and galleries were crowded with an audience anticipating a speech from Mr. Bright, who, on entering with the Mayor, was greeted with loud cheering.

The Mayor, on taking the chair, said he could conceive of no occasion when, as chief magistrate, he could take the chair with greater pleasure; and he did not think that his occupancy of the position of Mayor should preclude him from the expression of his private opinions. (Hear!) The object of the meeting had his entire sympathy. (Cheers.) They looked to the events transpiring in the Free States of America with the greatest interest, and, in some respects, with profound and solemn awe. Their desire was to show that they appreciated the practical proof of sympathy shown towards our suffering population in the noble gift that freighted the *George Griswold*, and which gave a contradiction to the calumnies uttered against the North by a portion of the people of this country. This act of the merchants of New York gave the lie to these vile statements alleging hatred to England. He was proud of this meeting, and of the presence of their illustrious townsman, Mr. Bright. (Cheers.)

Mr. Henry Kelsall moved the following resolution: —

"That the inhabitants of Rochdale, in public meeting assembled, the Mayor of the borough in the chair, do heartily thank the merchants of New York, and other citizens of the United States of America, who have generously contributed to the relief of the distress now so prevalent in this country; and they regard the supplies sent by the *George Griswold* and other ships as a proof of the Christian kindness and brotherly feeling of the people of the United States. They also take this occasion to express their earnest desire that peace may soon prevail on the American continent; and they will especially rejoice if that peace be accompanied by the Union re-established, with freedom secured to every man of every color within its vast dominion."

It would, he said, manifest great ingratitude if they did not suitably acknowledge this generous gift. It would be well if freedom, which was the birthright of every man, could be obtained without this bloodshed, and certainly he thought that the money spent upon the war would have been well applied to purchasing freedom for the slaves. (Hear! Hear!)

Alderman THOMAS ASHWORTH had great

pleasure in seconding the motion, and expressed a hope that all the acts of our government would give as much satisfaction as the command to honor the good laden ship as she entered the Mersey. (Hear!)

Mr. Bright, M. P., on being requested to support the resolution, was greeted with repeated plaudits. The honorable member said: —

Mr. Mayor, and fellow-townsmen, I feel as if we were in our places to-night, — (Hear!) — for we are met for the purpose of considering, and, I doubt not, of agreeing to a resolution expressive of our sense of the generosity of the merchants of New York, and other citizens of the United States, who have, in the midst of so many troubles and such great sacrifices, contributed to the relief of that appalling distress which has prevailed, and does still prevail, in this country.

I regard this transmission of assistance from the United States as a proof that the world moves onward in the direction of a better time. (Hear!) It is an evidence that, whatever may be the faults of ambitious men, and sometimes, may I not say, the crimes of governments, the peoples are drawing together, and beginning to learn that it never was intended that they should be hostile to each other, but that every nation should take a brotherly interest in every other nation in the world. (Cheers.) There has been, as we all know, not a little jealousy between some portions of the people of this country and some portions of the people of the United States. Perhaps the jealousy has existed more on this side. I think it has found more expression here, probably through the means of the public press, than has been the case with them. I am not alluding now to the last two years, but as long as most of us have been readers of newspapers and observers of what has passed around us.

The establishment of independence, eighty

years ago, the war of 1812, it may be occasionally the presumptuousness and the arrogance of a growing and prosperous nation on the other side of the Atlantic, — these things have stimulated ill-feeling and jealousy here, which have often found expression in language not of the very kindest character. But why should there be this jealousy between these two nations? Mr. Ashworth has said, and said very truly, "Are they not our own people?" I should think, as an Englishman, that to see that people so numerous, so powerful, so great in so many ways, should be to us a cause, not of envy or of fear, but rather of glory and rejoicing. (Hear!)

I have never visited the United States, but I can understand the pleasure with which an Englishman lands in a country three thousand miles off, and finds that every man he meets speaks his own language. (Hear!) I recollect some years ago reading a most amusing speech delivered by a Suffolk country gentleman, at a Suffolk agricultural dinner, I think it was, and I do not believe the speeches of Suffolk country gentlemen at Suffolk agricultural meetings are generally very amusing. (Laughter.) But this was a very amusing speech. This gentleman had travelled; he had been in the United States, and being intelligent enough to admire much that he saw there, he gave to his audience a description of some things that he had seen and observed; but that which seemed to delight him most was this, that when he stepped from the steamer on to the quay at New York, he said, "I found that everybody spoke Suffolk." (Laughter.) Now if anybody from this neighborhood should visit New York, I am afraid that he will not find everybody speaking Lancashire. (Laughter.) Our dialect, as you know, is vanishing into the past. It will be preserved to future times partly in the works of Tim Bobbin, — (laughter,) — but in a very much better and more instructive form in the admirable writings of one of my oldest and most valued friends, who is now, I suspect, upon this platform. (Cheers.) But if we should not find the people of New York speaking Lancashire, we should find them speaking English. (Cheers.) And if we followed a little further, and asked them what they read, we should find that they read all the books that we read that are worth reading, and a good many of their own, some of which have not yet reached us; that there are probably more readers in the United States of Milton, and Shakespeare, and Dryden, and Pope, and Byron, and Wordsworth, and Tennyson, than are to be found in this country; because, I think, it will probably be admitted by everybody who understands the facts of both countries, that, out of the twenty millions of population in the Free States of America, there are more persons who can read well than there are in the thirty millions of population of Great Britain and Ireland. (Hear!)

Well, if we leave their literature and turn

to their laws, we shall find that their laws have the same basis as ours, and that many of the great and memorable judgments of our greatest judges and lawyers are of high authority with them. If we come to that priceless possession which we have perhaps more clearly established than any other people in Europe, that of personal freedom, we shall find that in the Free States of America personal freedom is as much known, as well established, as fully appreciated, and as completely enjoyed as it is now in this country. And if we come to the form of their government, we shall find that it is in its principle, in its essence, not very dissimilar from that which our Constitution professes in this kingdom. The difference is this, that our Constitution has never yet been fully enjoyed by the people; the House in which forty-eight hours hence I may be sitting is not as full and fair and free a representation of the people, as is the House of Representatives that assembles at Washington. (Cheers.)

But, if there be differences, are there not great points of agreement, and are there any of these differences that justify us or them in regarding either nation as foreign or hostile?

Now, the people of Europe owe much more than they are often aware of to the Constitution of the United States of America, and to the existence of that great republic. The United States have been in point of fact an ark of refuge to the people of Europe fleeing from the storms and the revolutions of the old continent. (Hear!) They have been, as far as the artisans and laboring population of this country are concerned, a lifeboat to them; and they have saved hundreds of thousands of men and of families from disastrous shipwreck. (Hear!) The existence of that free country and free government has had a prodigious influence upon freedom in Europe and in England; and if you could have before you a chart of the condition of Europe when the United States became a nation, and another chart of the condition of Europe now, you would see the difference, the enormous stride which has been made in Europe; and you may rely upon it that not a little of it has been occasioned by the influence of the great example of that country, free in its political institutions beyond all other countries, and yet maintaining its course in peace, preserving order, and conferring upon all its people a degree of prosperity which in these old countries is not yet known. (Cheers.)

I should like now to speak specially to the workingmen who are here, who have no capital but their skill and their industry and their bodily strength. In fifteen years, from 1845 to 1860,—and this is a fact which I stated in this room more than a year ago, when speaking on the question of America, but it is a fact which every workingman ought to have in his mind always when he is considering what America is,—in fifteen years there have emigrated to the United

States from Great Britain and Ireland not less than two million four hundred thousand persons. (Hear! Hear!) Millions are easily spoken, not easily counted, with great difficulty comprehended; but the twenty-four hundred thousand persons that I have described means a population equal to not less than sixty towns, every one of them of the size and population of Rochdale. (Hear!) And every one of these men who have emigrated, as he crossed the Atlantic, — if he went by steam, a fortnight, and if he went by sails, only a month or five weeks, — found himself in a country where to his senses a vast revolution had taken place, comprehending all that men anticipate from any kind of revolution that shall advance political and social equality in their own land, — a revolution which commenced in the War of Independence, which has been going on, and which has been confirmed by all that has transpired in subsequent years.

He does not find that he belongs to what

is called the "lower classes"; he is not shut out from any of the rights of citizenship; he is admitted to the full enjoyment of all political privileges, as far as they are extended to any portion of the population; and he has there advantages which the people of this country have not yet gained, because we are but gradually making our way out of the darkness and the errors and the tyrannies of past ages. (Hear!) But in America he finds the land not cursed with feudalism,—(Hear!)—it is free to every man to buy and sell and possess and transmit. (Hear!) He finds in the town in which he lives that the noblest buildings are the school-houses to which his children are freely admitted. (Hear!) And among those twenty millions,—for I am now confining my observations to the Free States,—the son of every man has easy admission to school, has fair opportunity for improvement, and, if God has gifted him with power of head and of heart, there is nothing of usefulness, nothing of greatness, nothing of success, in that country, to which he may not fairly aspire.

And, sir, this makes a difference between that country and this, on which I must say another word. One of the most painful things to my mind to be seen in England is this, that amongst the great body of those classes which earn their living by their daily labor, — it is particularly observable in the agricultural districts, and it is too much to be observed even in our districts, — there is an absence of that hope which every man ought to have in his soul that there is for him, if he be industrious and frugal, a comfortable independence as he advances in life. (Cheers.) In the United States that hope prevails everywhere, because everywhere there is an open career; there is no privileged class; there is complete education extended to all, and every man feels that he was not born to be in penury and in suffering, but that by his honest efforts there is no point in the social ladder to which he may not fairly hope to raise himself. (Cheers.)

Well, looking at all this, — and I have but touched on some very prominent points, — I should say that it offers to us every motive, not for fear, not for jealousy, not for hatred, but rather for admiration, gratitude, and friendship. (Cheers.) I am persuaded of this as much as I am of anything that I know or believe, that the more perfect the friendship that is established between the people of England and the free people of America, the more you will find your path of progress here made easy for you, and the more will social and political liberty advance amongst us. (Loud cheers, and a little interruption, from the very crowded state of the room, respecting which Mr. Bright remarked, "Our Public Hall is not big enough.")

But this country which I have been in part describing is now the scene of one of the greatest calamities that can afflict mankind. (Hear!) After seventy years of almost uninterrupted peace, that country has become the scene of a war more gigantic, perhaps, than any that we have any record of with regard to any other nation, or any other people; for the scene of this warfare is so extended as to reach in distance almost across Europe. At this very moment military operations are being undertaken at points as distant from each other as Madrid is distant from Moscow. But this great strife cannot have arisen amongst an educated and intelligent people without some great and overruling cause. Let us for a moment examine that cause, and let us ask ourselves whether it is possible at such a time to stand neutral in regard to the contending parties, and to refuse our sympathy to one or the other of them. (Hear! Hear!) I find men sometimes who profess a strict neutrality; they wish neither the one thing nor the other. This arises either from the fact that they are profoundly ignorant with regard to this matter, — (Hear!) — or else that they sympathize with the South, but are rather ashamed to admit it. (Cheers, and laughter.)

There are two questions concerned in this struggle; hitherto, generally, one has only been discussed. There is the question whether negro slavery shall continue to be adopted amongst Christian nations, or whether it shall be entirely abolished. (Hear!) Because, bear in mind that if the result of the struggle that is now proceeding in America should abolish slavery within the territories of the United States, then soon after slavery in Brazil, and slavery in Cuba, will also fall. (Hear!) I was speaking the other day to a gentleman, well acquainted with Cuban affairs; he is often in the habit of seeing persons who come from Cuba to this country on business; and I asked him what his Cuban friends said of what was going on in America. He said, "They speak of it with the greatest apprehension; all the property of Cuba," he said, "is based on slavery; and they say that if slavery comes to an end in America, as they believe it will, through this war, slavery will have a very short life in Cuba." Therefore, the question that is being now tried is not merely whether four millions of slaves in America shall be free, but whether the vast number of slaves (I know not the number) in Cuba and Brazil shall also be liberated. (Hear!)

But there is another question besides that of the negro, and which to you whom I am now addressing is scarcely less important. I say that the question of freedom to men of all races is deeply involved in this great strife in the United States. (Cheers.) I said I wanted the workingmen of this audience to listen to my statement, because it is to them I particularly wish to address myself. I say, that not only is the question of negro slavery concerned in this struggle, but, if we are to take the opinion of leading writers and men in the Southern States of America, the freedom of white men is not safe in their hands. (Hear!) Now, I will not trouble you with pages of extracts which would confirm all that I am about to say, but I shall read you two or three short ones that will explain exactly what I mean.

The city of Richmond, as you know, is the capital of what is called the Southern Confederacy. In that city a newspaper is published, called the *Richmond Examiner*, which is one of the most able, and perhaps about the most influential, paper published in the Slave States. Listen to what the *Richmond Examiner* says: — "The experiment of universal liberty has failed. The evils of free society are insufferable. Free society in the long run is impracticable; it is everywhere starving, demoralizing, and insurrectionary. Policy and humanity alike forbid the extension of its evils to new peoples and to coming generations; and therefore free society must fall and give way to a slave society, — a social system old as the world, universal as man."

Well, on another occasion, the same paper treats this subject in this way. The writer says: "Hitherto the defence of slavery has encountered great difficulties, because its apologists stopped half-way. They confined the defence of slavery to negro slavery alone, abandoning the principle of slavery, and admitting that every other form of slavery was wrong. Now the line of defence is changed. The South maintains that slavery is just, natural, and necessary, and that it does not depend on the difference of complexions." (Cries of "Shame!")

But following up this is an extract from a speech by a Mr. Cobb, who is an eminent man in Southern politics and in Southern opinion. He says: "There is, perhaps, no solution of the great problem of reconciling the interests of labor and capital, so as to protect each from the encroachments and oppressions of the other, so simple and effective as negro slavery. By making the laborer himself capital, the conflict ceases, and the interests become identical." (Shame!)

Now, I do not know whether there is any workingman here who does not fully or partly realize the meaning of those extracts. They mean this, that if a man in this neighborhood,—(for they pity us very much in our benighted condition as regards capital and labor, and they have an admirable way in their view of putting an end to strikes,)—they say that, if a man in this neighborhood had ten thousand pounds sterling in a cotton or woollen factory, and he employed a hundred men, women, and children, that instead of paying them whatever wages had been agreed upon, allowing them to go to the other side of the town, and work where they liked, or to move to another county, or to emigrate to America, or to have any kind of will or wish whatever with regard to their own disposal, that they should be to him capital, just the same as the horses are in his stable; that he should sell the husband

South, — "South" in America means something very dreadful to the negro, — that they should sell the wife if they liked, that they should sell the children, that, in point of fact, they should do whatsoever they liked with them, and that, if any one of them resisted any punishment which the master chose to inflict, the master should be held justified if he beat his slaves to death; and that not one of those men should have the power to give evidence in any court of justice, in any case, against a white man, however much he might have suffered from that white man. (Hear!)

Now you will observe that this most important paper in the South writes for that principle, and this eminent Southern politician indorses it, and thinks it a cure for all the evils which exist in the Old World, and in the Northern and Free States; and there is not a paper in the South, nor is there a man as eminent or more eminent than Mr. Cobb, who has dared to write or speak in condemnation of the atrocity of that language. (Hear!) I believe this great strife to have had its origin in an infamous conspiracy against the rights of human nature. (Hear!) Those principles, which they distinctly avow and proclaim, are not to be found, as far as I know, in the pages of any heathen writer of old times, nor are they to be discovered in the teachings or the practice of savage nations in our times. It is the doctrine of devils, and not of men (Hear! Hear!); and all mankind should shudder at the enormity of the guilt which the leaders of this conspiracy have brought upon that country. (Loud applause.)

Now, let us look at two or three facts, which I take to be very remarkable, on the surface of the case, but which there are men in this country, and I am told they may be found even in this town, who altogether ignore and deny. The war was not commenced by those to whom your resolution refers; it was commenced by the South;

they rebelled against the majority. It was not a rebellion against a monarchy, or an aristocracy, or some other form of government which has its hold upon people, sometimes by services, but often from tradition; but it was against a government of their own, and a compact of their own, that they violently rebelled, and for the expressed and avowed purpose of maintaining the institution of slavery, and for the purpose, not disavowed, of reopening the slave-trade, and, as these extracts show, if their principles should be fully carried out, of making bondage universal among all classes of laborers and artisans. When I say that their object was to reopen the slave-trade, do not for a moment imagine that I am overstating the case against them. They argue, with a perfect logic, that, if slavery was right, the slave-trade could not be wrong; if the slave-trade be wrong, slavery cannot be right; and that if it be lawful and moral to go to the State of Virginia and buy a slave for two thousand dollars, and take him to Louisiana, it would not be wrong to go to Africa, and buy a slave for fifty dollars, and take him to Louisiana. That was their argument; it is an argument to this day, and is an argument that in my opinion no man can controvert; and the lawful existence of slavery is as a matter of course to be followed, and would be followed, wherever there was the power, by the reopening of the traffic in negroes from Africa. (Hear!)

That is not all these people have done. Reference has been made, in the resolution and in the speeches, to the distress which prevails in this district, and you are told, and have been told over and over again, that all this distress has arisen from the blockade of the ports of the Southern States. There is at least one great port from which in past times two millions of bales of cotton a year have found their way to Europe, — the port of New Orleans, — which is blockaded; and the United States government has proclaimed that any cotton that is sent from the interior to New Orleans for shipment, although it belongs to persons in arms against the government, shall yet be permitted to go to Europe, and they shall receive unmolested the proceeds of the sale of that cotton. But still the cotton does not come. The reason why it does not come is not because it would do harm to the United States government for it to come, or that it would in any way assist the United States government in carrying on the war. The reason that it does not come is, because its being kept back is supposed to be a way of influencing public opinion in England, and the course of the English government in reference to the American war. (Cheers.) They burn the cotton that they may injure us, and they injure us because they think that we cannot live even for a year without their cotton; and that to get it we should send ships of war, break the blockade, make war upon the North, and assist the slave-owners to maintain, or to obtain, their independence.

Now, with regard to the question of American cotton, one or two extracts will be sufficient; but I would give you a whole pamphlet of them if it were necessary. Mr. Mann, an eminent person in the State of Georgia, says: "With the failure of the cotton, England fails. Stop her supply of Southern slave-grown cotton, and her factories stop, her commerce stops, the healthful normal circulation of her life-blood stops." Again he says: "In one year from the stoppage of England's supply of Southern slave-grown cotton, the Chartists would be in all her streets and fields, revolution would be rampant throughout the island, and nothing that is would exist." He also says, addressing an audience: "Why, sirs, British lords hold their lands, British bishops hold their revenues, Victoria holds her sceptre, by the grace of cotton, as surely as by the grace of God." (Roars of laughter.) Senator Wigfall says, "If we stop the supply of cotton for one week, England would be starving. (Laughter.) Queen Victoria's crown would not stand on her head one week, if the supply of cotton was stopped; nor would her head stand on her shoulders." (Repeated laughter.) Mr. Stephens, who is the Vice-President of the Southern Confederacy, says: "There will be revolution in Europe, there will be starvation there; our cotton is the element that will do it." (Loud laughter.)

Now, I am not stating the mere result of any discovery of my own, but it would be impossible to read the papers of the South, or the speeches made in the South, before, and at the time of, and after the secession, without seeing that the universal opinion there was, that the stoppage of the supply of cotton would be our instantaneous ruin, and that if they could only lay hold of it, keep it back in the country, or burn it, so that it never could be used, that then the people of Lancashire, merchants, manufacturers, and operatives in mills, — everybody dependent upon this vast industry, — would immediately arise and protest against the English government abstaining for one moment from recognition of the South and war with the North, and a resolution to do the utmost that we could to create a Southern slave independent republic. (Cheers.)

And these very men who have been wishing to drag us into a war that would have covered us with everlasting infamy, — (loud cheers,) — they have sent their envoys to this country, Mr. Yancey, and Mr. Mann (I don't know whether or not the same Mr. Mann to whom I have been referring), and Mr. Mason, the author of the Fugitive Slave Law. (Hear! Hear!) And these men have been in this country; one of them, I believe, is here now, envoys sent to be friends with the Queen of England, to be received at her court, and to make friends with the great men in London. They come, — I have seen them under the gallery of the House of

Commons, and members of the House shaking hands with them and congratulating them if there has been some military success on their side, and receiving them as if they were here from the most honorable government, and with the most honorable mission. Why, the thing which they have broken off from the United States to maintain, is felony by your law. (Cheers.) They are not only slave owners, slave buyers and sellers, but that which out of Pandemonium itself never before was conceived of, — they are slave breeders for the slave market; and these men have come to your country, and are to be met with at elegant tables in London, and are in fast friendship with some of your public men, and are constantly found in some of your newspaper offices; and they are here to ask Englishmen — Englishmen with a history for freedom — to join hands with their atrocious conspiracy. (Prolonged and repeated cheering.)

I regret more than I have words to express this painful fact, that of all the countries in Europe this country is the only one which has men in it who are willing to take active steps in favor of this intended slave government. We supply the ships; we supply the arms, the munitions of war; we give aid and comfort to this foulest of all crimes. Englishmen only do it. In the newspapers I believe you have not seen a single statement that any French, or Belgian, or Dutch, or Russian ship has been engaged in, or seized whilst attempting to violate the blockade, and to carry arms to the South. (Cheers.) They are English liberal newspapers only, which support this stupendous iniquity.— They are English statesmen only, who profess to be liberal, who have said a word in favor of the authors of this now-enacting revolution in America.

The other day, not a week since, a member of the present government,—he is not a statesman,—he is the son of a great statesman,—(Hear!)—and occupies the position of Secretary for Ireland,—he dared to say to an English audience that he wished the Republic to be divided, (hisses,) and that the South should become an independent state. Why, if that island which—I suppose in punishment for some of its offences—has been committed to his care,—(laughter, and cheers,)—if that island were to attempt to secede, not to set up a slave kingdom, but a kingdom more free than it has ever yet been, the government of which he is a member would sack its cities and drench its soil with blood before they would allow this kingdom to be established. (Immense cheering; and a voice, "Bright forever!" followed by renewed cheering.)

But the workingmen of England, and I will say it too for the great body of the middle classes of England, they have not been wrong upon this great question. As for you,—men laboring from morn till night that you may honorably and honestly maintain your families, and the independence of your households,—you are too slowly emerging from a condition of things far from independent,—far from free,—for you to have sympathy with this fearful crime which I have been describing. (Cheers.) You come, as it were, from bonds yourselves, and you can sympathize with them who are still in bondage. (Cheers.)

See that meeting that was held in Manchester a month ago, in the Free Trade Hall, of five thousand or six thousand men. See the address which they there carried unanimously to the President of the United States. See that meeting held the other night in Exeter Hall, in London; that vast room, the greatest room, I suppose, in the Metropolis, filled so much that its overflowings filled another large room in the same building, and when that was full, the further overflowings filled the street; and in both rooms, and in the street, speeches were made on this great question. But what is said by the writers in this infamous Southern press in this country with regard to that meeting? Who was there? "A gentleman who had written a novel, and two or three Dissenting ministers."

Well, I shall not attempt any defence of those gentlemen. What they do, they do openly, in the face of day; and if they utter sentiments on this question, it is from a public platform, with thousands of their countrymen gazing into their faces. These men who slander them write behind a mask,—(Hear!)—and, what is more, they dare not tell in the open day that which they write in the columns of their journal. (Cheers.) But if it be true, now, that there is nothing in the writer of a successful novel, or in two or three pious and noble-minded Dissenting ministers, to collect a great audience, what does it prove, if there was a great audience? It only proves that they were not collected by the reputation of any orator who was expected to address them, but by their cordial and ardent sympathy for the great cause which was laid before them. (Loud cheers.)

Everybody now that I meet says to me, "Public opinion seems to have undergone a considerable change." (Laughter.) The fact is, people don't know very much about America. They are learning more every day. They have been greatly misled by what are called "the best public instructors." (Laughter.) Jefferson, who was one of the greatest men that the United States have produced, said that newspapers should be divided into four compartments, in one of them they should print the true; in the next, the probable; in the third, the possible; and in the fourth, the lies. (Laughter, and cheers.) With regard to some of these newspapers, I incline to think, as far as their leading columns go, that an equal division of space would be found very inconvenient, — (loud cheers,) — and that the last-named compartment, when dealing with American questions, would have to be at least four times as large as the first. (Cheers.)

Coming back to the question of this war: I admit, of course, — everybody must admit, — that we are not responsible for it, for its commencement, or for the manner in which it is carried out; nor can we be very clearly, or in any considerable degree, responsible for its result. But there is one thing which we are responsible for, and that is for our sympathies, for the manner in which we regard it, and for the tone which we take when we discuss it. What shall we say, then, with regard to it? On which side shall we stand? I don't believe it is possible to be strictly, coldly neutral. The question at issue is too great, the contest is too grand in the eye of the world. It is impossible for any man, who can have an opinion worth anything on any question, not to have some kind of an opinion on the question of this war. I am not ashamed of my opinion, or of the sympathy which I feel, and have over and over again expressed, on the side of the free North. I cannot understand how any man witnessing what is enacting on the American continent can employ himself with small cavils against the free people of the North, and close his eye entirely to the enormity of the purposes of the South. I cannot understand how any Englishman, who in past years has been accustomed to say that "there was one foul blot upon the fair fame of the American Republic," can now express any sympathy for those who would perpetuate and extend that blot. And, more, if we profess to be, though it be with imperfect and faltering steps, the followers of Him who declared it to be his Divine mission "to heal the broken-hearted, to preach deliverance to the captives and recovering of sight to the blind, to set at liberty them that are bruised," — must we not reject with indignation and scorn the proffered alliance and friendship with a power based on human bondage, and which contemplates the overthrow and the extinction of the dearest rights of the most helpless of mankind? (Cheers.)

If we are the friends of freedom,—personal and political,—and we all profess to be that, and most of us, more or less, are striving after it more completely for our country,—how can we withhold our sympathy from a government and a people amongst whom white men have always been free, and who are now offering an equal freedom to the black? I advise you not to believe in the "destruction" of the American nation. If facts should happen by any chance to force you to believe it, don't commit the crime of wishing it. (Cheers.) I don't blame men who draw different conclusions from mine from the facts, and who believe that the restoration of the Union is impossible. We can only use our own sense more or less as we may have it upon the facts before us. But I blame those men that wish for such a catastrophe. For myself, I have never despaired, and I will not despair. In the language of one of our old poets, who wrote, I think, more than three hundred years ago, I will not despair, —

> "For I have seen a ship in haven fall,
> After the storm had broke both mast and shroud."

From the very outburst of this great convulsion, I have had but one hope and one faith, and it was this: that the result of this stupendous strife might be to make freedom the heritage forever of a whole continent, and that the grandeur and the prosperity of the American Union might never be impaired. (The honorable member resumed his seat amid enthusiastic cheering.)

The first resolution was then submitted to the meeting, and carried amidst great applause.

Mr. Alderman Livsey next moved: —

That a copy of the foregoing resolution be signed by the Mayor, and be forwarded to the Chairman of the New York Relief Committee.

Mr. J. Petrie, Jr., in seconding this resolution, remarked that he felt it no small honor to be permitted to take part in the proceedings of this meeting. Mr. Bright in less than forty-eight hours would take his place in the House of Commons, and he would be able to bear testimony to the enthusiasm, unity, and determination of the inhabitants of Rochdale in reference to the American struggle. (Cheers.)

The resolution was carried with acclamation.

Mr. Alderman Healey proposed a vote of thanks to the Mayor for so ably filling the chair. The motion was seconded by Mr. R. Hurst, and passed.

Before the meeting separated, three cheers were given for Mr. Bright, and followed by hearty cheers for Mr. Lincoln.

THE STRUGGLE IN AMERICA

IN RELATION TO THE WORKINGMEN OF BRITAIN.

Address at a Meeting of the Trades' Unions of London in St. James's Hall, March 26, 1863, with the Resolutions and Address to President Lincoln.

A MEETING convened by the Trades' Unions of London took place on the 26th ultimo, at St. James's Hall, Piccadilly, for the purpose of expressing sympathy with the Northern States of America in the present struggle, and a belief that their success would lead to the speedy emancipation of the negro race. Whatever might otherwise have been the case, the announcement that the honorable member for Birmingham would take the chair was sufficient to account for an attendance so numerous as to tax the power of accommodation of the vast hall to the utmost extent.

Among those present on the platform were Mr. Stansfeld, M. P., Mr. Lawson, M. P., Mr. John Stuart Mill, Mr. P. A. Taylor, M. P., Rev. Newman Hall, Professor Beesly, etc.

Mr. Bright, on making his appearance, was hailed with loud and long-continued cheering, which was renewed on his rising to commence the business of the evening. The honorable gentleman, who was suffering from a severe cold, spoke as follows: —

When the committee did me the honor to ask me to attend this meeting to-night and to take the chair, I felt that I was not at liberty to refuse, for I considered that there was something remarkable in the character of this meeting; and I need not tell you that the cause which we are assembled to discuss is one which excites my warmest sympathies. (Cheers.) This meeting is remarkable, inasmuch as it is not what is commonly called a public meeting, but it is a meeting, as you have seen by the announcements and advertisements by which it has been called — it is a meeting of members of Trades' Unions and Trades' Societies in London. The members of these societies have not usually stepped out from their ordinary business to take part in meetings of this kind on public questions.

The subject which we have met to discuss is one of surpassing interest, — which excites at this moment, and has excited for two years past, the attention and the astonishment of the civilized world. We see a country which for many years — during the lifetime of the oldest amongst us — has been the most peaceful, and prosperous, and most free, amongst the great nations of the earth, — (Hear! Hear!) — we see it plunged at once into the midst of a sanguinary revolution, whose proportions are so gigantic as to dwarf all other revolutionary records and events of which we have any knowledge. But I do not wonder at this revolution. No man can read the history of the United States from the time when they ceased to be dependent Colonies of England, without discovering that at the birth of that great Republic there was sown the seed of its dissolution, or at least of its extreme peril; and the infant giant in its cradle may be said to have been rocked under the shadow of the cypress, which is the symbol of mortality and the tomb. (Cheers.)

Colonial weakness, when face to face with British strength, made it impossible to put an end to slavery, or to establish a republic free from slavery. To meet England, it was necessary to be united, and to be united it was necessary to tolerate slavery; and from that hour to this, — at least to a period within the last two or three years, — the love of the Union and the patriotism of the American people have induced them constantly to make concessions to slavery, because they knew that when they ceased to make these concessions they ran the peril of that disruption which has now arrived; and they dreaded the destruction of their country even more than they hated the evil of slavery. (Hear!) But these concessions failed, as I believe concessions to evil always do fail. These concessions failed to secure safety in that Union. There were principles at war which were wholly irreconcilable. The South, as you know, for fifty years has been engaged in building fresh ramparts by which it may defend its institutions. The North has been growing yearly greater in freedom; and though the conflict might be postponed, it was obviously inevitable.

In our day, then, that which the statesmen of America had hoped permanently to postpone has arrived. The great trial is now going on in the sight of the world, and the verdict upon this great question must at last be rendered. But how much is at stake? Some men in this country, some writers, treat it as if, after all, it was no great matter that had caused this contest in the United States. I say that a whole continent is at stake. (Cheers.) It is not a question of boundary;

it is not a question of tariff; it is not a question of supremacy of party, or even of the condition of four millions of negroes. (Cheers.) It is more than that. It is a question of a whole continent, with its teeming millions, and what shall be their present and their future fate. (Cheers.) It is for these millions freedom or slavery, education or ignorance, light or darkness, Christian morality, ever widening and all-blessing in its influence, or an overshadowing and all-blasting guilt. (Cheers.)

There are men, good men, who say that we in England, who are opposed to war, should take no public part in this great question. Only yesterday I received from a friend of mine, whose fidelity I honor, a letter, in which he asked me whether I thought, with the views which he supposed I entertain on the question of war, it was fitting that I should appear at such a meeting as this. It is not our war; we did not make it. We deeply lament it. (Hear!) It is not in our power to bring it to a close; but I know not that we are called upon to shut our eyes and to close our hearts to the great issues which are depending upon it. Now we are meeting to ask one another some questions. Has England any opinion with regard to this American question? Has England any sympathy, on one side or the other, with either party in this great struggle? But, to come nearer, I would ask whether this meeting has any opinion upon it, and whether our sympathies have been stirred in relation to it? It is true, to this meeting not many rich, not many noble, have been called. It is a meeting composed of artisans and workingmen of the city of London, — men whose labor, in combination with capital and directing skill, has built this great city, and has made England great. (Hear! and cheers.) I address myself to these men. I ask them, — I ask you, — have you any special interest in this contest?

Privilege thinks it has a great interest in

it, and every morning, with blatant voice, it comes into your streets and curses the American Republic. (Cheers.) Privilege has beheld an afflicting spectacle for many years past. It has beheld thirty millions of men, happy and prosperous, without emperor, (cheers,) without king, (cheers,) without the surroundings of a court, (cheers,) without nobles, except such as are made by eminence in intellect and virtue, (cheers,) without state bishops and state priests,—

"Sole venders of the lore which works salvation,"—

without great armies and great navies, without great debt and without great taxes. (Hear!) Privilege has shuddered at what might happen to old Europe if this grand experiment should succeed. (Cheers.) But you, the workers,—you, striving after a better time,—you, struggling upwards towards the light, with slow and painful steps,—you have no cause to look with jealousy upon a country which, amongst all the great nations of the globe, is that one where labor has met with the highest honor, and where it has reaped its greatest reward. (Cheers.) Are you aware of the fact, that in fifteen years, which is but as yesterday when it is past, two and a half millions of your countrymen have found a home in the United States, — (Hear!) — that a population equal nearly, if not quite, to the population of this great city — itself equal to no mean kingdom — has emigrated from these shores? In the United States there has been, as you know, an open door for every man, — (Hear!) — and millions have entered into it, and have found rest.

Now, take the two sections of the country which are engaged in this fearful struggle. In the one, labor is honored more than elsewhere in the world; there, more than in any other country, men rise to competence and independence; a career is open; the pursuit of happiness is not hopelessly thwarted by the law. In the other section of that country, labor is not only not honored, but it is degraded. (Hear! Hear!) The laborer is made a chattel. He is no more his own than the horse that drags an omnibus through the next street; nor is his wife, nor is his child, nor is anything that is his, his own. (Hear!) And if you have not heard the astounding statement, it may be as well for a moment to refer to it, — that it is not black men only who should be slaves. Only to-day, I read from one of the Southern papers a statement that — "Slavery in the Jewish times was not the slavery of negroes; and therefore, if you confine slavery to negroes, you lose your sheet-anchor, which is the Bible argument in favor of slavery." (Hear!)

I think nothing can be more fitting for the discussion of the members of the Trade Societies of London. You in your Trade Societies help each other when you are sick, or if you meet with accidents. You do many kind acts amongst each other. You have other business also; you have to maintain what you believe to be the just rights of industry and of your separate trades; and sometimes, as you know, you do things which many people do not approve, and which, probably, when you come to think more coolly of them, you may even doubt the wisdom of yourselves. That is only saying that you are not immaculate, and that your wisdom, like the wisdom of other classes, is not absolutely perfect. But they have in the Southern States a specific for all the differences between capital and labor. They say, "Make the laborer capital; the free system in Europe is a rotten system; let us get rid of that, and make all the laborers as much capital and as much the property of the capitalist and employer as the capitalist's cattle and horses are property, and then the whole system will move with that perfect ease and harmony which the world admires so much in the Southern States of America." (Cheers and laughter.) I believe there never was a question submitted to the public opinion of the world which it was more becoming the working-men and members of Trades' Unions and Trade Societies of every kind in this country fully to consider, than this great question. (Hear!)

But there may be some in this room, and there are some who say to me, "But what is to become of our trade? What is to become of the capitalist and the laborer of Lancashire?" I am not sure that much of the capital of Lancashire will not be ruined. I am not sure that very large numbers of its population will not have to remove to seek other employment, either in this or some other country. I am not one of those who underrate this great calamity. On the contrary, I have scarcely met with any man,—not more than half a dozen,—since this distress in our county began, who has been willing to measure the magnitude of this calamity according to the scale with which I have viewed it.

But let us examine this question. The

distress of Lancashire comes from failure of supply of cotton. The failure of the supply of cotton comes from the war in the United States. The war in the United States has originated in the effort of the slaveholders of that country to break up what they themselves admit to be the freest and best government that ever existed, for the sole purpose of making perpetual the institution of slavery. (Cheers.) But if the South began the war, and created all the mischief, does it look reasonable that we should pat them on the back, and be their friends? (No! No!) If they have destroyed cotton, or withheld it, shall we therefore take them to our bosoms?

I have a letter written by an agent in the city of Nashville, who had been accustomed to buy cotton there before the war, and who returned there immediately after that city came into the possession of the Northern forces. He began his trade, and cotton came in. Not Union planters only, but Secession planters, began to bring in the produce of their plantations, and he had a fair chance of re-establishing his business; but the moment this was discovered by the commanders of the Southern forces at some distance from the city, then they issued the most peremptory orders that every boat-load of cotton on the rivers, every wagon-load upon the roads, and every car-load upon the railroads, that was leaving any plantations for the purposes of sale, should be immediately destroyed. The result was, that the cotton trade was at once again put an end to, and I believe only to a very small extent has it been reopened, even to this hour.

Then take the state of New Orleans, which, as you know, has been now for many months in the possession of the Northern forces. The Northern commanders there had issued announcements that any cotton sent down to New Orleans for exportation, even though it came from the most resolved friends of secession in the district, should still be safe. It might be purchased to ship to Europe, and the proceeds of that cotton might be returned, and the trade be reopened. But you have not found cotton come down to New Orleans, although its coming there under those terms would be of no advantage, particularly to the North. It has been withheld with this single object, to create in the manufacturing districts of France and England a state of suffering that might at last become unbearable, and thus compel the government, in spite of all that international law may teach, in spite of all that morality may enjoin upon them, to take sides with the South, and go to war with the North for the sake of liberating whatever cotton there is now in the plantations of the Secession States. (Hear!)

At this moment, such of you as read the city articles of the daily papers will see that a loan has been contracted for in the city, to the amount of three millions sterling, on behalf of the Southern Confederacy. (Shame!)

It is not brought into the market by any firm with an English name; but I am sorry to be obliged to believe that many Englishmen have taken portions of that loan. Now the one great object of that loan is this, to pay in this country for vessels which are being built, — Alabamas, — from which it is hoped that so much irritation will arise in the minds of the people of the Northern States, that England may be dragged into war to take sides with the South and with slavery. (Hear!) The South was naturally hostile to England, because England was hostile to slavery. Now the great hope of the insurrection has been from the beginning, that Englishmen would not have fortitude to bear the calamities which it has brought upon us; but by some trick or by some accident we might be brought into a war with the North, and therefore give strength to the South. (Hear! Hear!)

I should hope that this question is now so plain that most Englishmen must understand it; and least of all do I expect that the six millions of men in the United Kingdom who are not enfranchised have any doubt upon it. Their instincts are always in the main right, and if they get the facts and information, I can rely on their influence being put in the right scale. I wish I could state what would be as satisfactory to myself with regard to some others. There may be men outside, there are men sitting amongst your legislators, who will build and equip corsair ships—(Hear! Hear!)—to prey upon the commerce of a friendly power,—who will disregard the laws and honor of their country,—who will trample on the proclamation of their sovereign,—and who, for the sake of the glittering profit which sometimes waits on crime, are content to cover themselves with everlasting infamy. There may be men, too,—rich men,—in this city of London, who will buy in the slave-owners' loan, and who, for the chance of more gain than honest dealing will afford them, will help a conspiracy whose fundamental institution, whose corner-stone, is declared to be felony, and infamous by the statutes of their country. (Cheers.)

I speak not to those men, — I leave them to their conscience in that hour which cometh to all of us, when conscience speaks and the soul is no longer deaf to her voice. I speak to you, the workingmen of London, the representatives, as you are here to-night, of the feelings and the interests of the millions who cannot hear my voice. (Cheers.) I wish you to be true to yourselves. Dynasties may fail, aristocracies may perish, privilege will vanish into the dim past; but you, your children, and your children's children will remain, and from you the English people will be continued to succeeding generations.

You wish the freedom of your country. You wish it for yourselves. You strive for it in many ways. Do not then give the hand of fellowship to the worst foes of freedom that the world has ever seen, and do not, I beseech you, bring down a curse upon your cause which no after penitence can ever lift from it. (Cheers.) You will not do this. (Cries of Never!) I have faith in you. Impartial history will tell that, when your statesmen were hostile or coldly neutral, when many of your rich men were corrupt, when your press — which ought to have instructed and defended — was mainly written to betray, the fate of a continent and of its vast population being in peril, you clung to freedom with an unfaltering trust that God in his infinite mercy will yet make it the heritage of all his children. (Loud cheers.)

Mr. Howell, a bricklayer, then proposed the first resolution, which was as follows: —

"That the attempt of the American slave-owners to break up the Union, in which their liberties and constitutional rights had never been interfered with, is destructive of the first principles of political society, and that this meeting regards with indignation the conduct of these public men, capitalists and journalists in this country, who have abetted the cause of the Confederates; and, further, that the government of this country, in permitting the pirate ship Alabama to leave Liverpool, was guilty of negligence, and has failed in its duty to a friendly nation."

Mr. RODGERS, a shoemaker, and Mr. MANTZ, a compositor, seconded it, after which it was put to the meeting, and carried unanimously.

Mr. W. R. CREMER, a joiner, moved, Professor BEESLY seconded, and Mr. CONOLLY, a mason, supported the second resolution, which was to the following effect:—

"That we altogether repudiate the statements that the war now raging in America is the result of republican or democratic institutions, but rather do we believe that the liberty arising out of such institutions has made it impossible for slavery longer to exist there; and we further believe, that, should the South be successful in setting up a government founded on human slavery, to recognize such a government would be to take a step backwards in civilization; and we declare that we will use our utmost efforts to prevent the recognition of any government founded on such a monstrous iniquity. And we hereby tender our thanks to the President, government, and people of the Northern States for the firmness they have displayed, and the sacrifices they have made to restore the Union, and to consolidate the liberty of the Republic; and as the cause of labor and liberty is one all over the world, we bid them God speed in their glorious work of emancipation."

This being put to the meeting, was also carried unanimously.

The following address to President Lincoln, embodying these views, was then unanimously adopted, with the understanding that a committee of the Trades' Unions should present it to Mr. Adams, the United States Minister, for transmission to Washington.

"To Abraham Lincoln,
President of the United States of America.

"Honored Sir:—A portion of the British press, led by the infamous *Times*, an arrogant aristocracy, and some of the moneyed classes of this country, having misrepresented the wishes and feelings of its people with regard to the lamentable contest between two portions of the great Republic, of which you are the legal and constitutional chief, — we, the Trades' Unionists and workingmen of London, in public meeting assembled, desire to assure you and the people of the Northern and loyal States of

America, that our earnest and heartfelt sympathies are with you in the arduous struggle you are maintaining in the cause of human freedom. We indignantly protest against the assertion that the people of England wish for the success of the Southern States in their diabolical attempt to establish a separate government on the basis of human slavery. However much a liberty-hating aristocracy and an unscrupulous moneyocracy may desire the consummation of such a crime, we, the workingmen of London, view it with abhorrence.

"We know that slavery in America must have an indirect but real tendency to degrade and depress labor in this country also, and for this, if for no higher reason, we should refuse our sympathy to this infamous Rebellion. The history of our race has been the story of a long-continued struggle for freedom; and we prize too highly the liberties bequeathed us by our fathers to desecrate their memories by descending to associate with the conspirators who seek to sink the producers of human necessaries and human wealth into soulless beasts. Though we have felt proud of our country, of the freedom won for its children, by the sacrifices and the blood of our fathers, yet have we ever turned with glowing admiration to your great Republic, where a higher political and social freedom has been generally established; but we have always regretted that its citizens, our brothers in the great Anglo-Saxon family, should have allowed the foul stain of negro slavery to remain a black spot on their otherwise noble institutions.

"When you, sir, were elected chief magistrate of the great American Republic, we hoped for the inauguration of a policy which should cause slavery to disappear from the soil of the United States, and we have not been disappointed. Though surrounded by difficulties, though trammelled by enactments made during the ascendency of the slave-owners, you have struck off the shackles from the poor slaves of Columbia; you have welcomed as men, as equals under God, the colored peoples of Hayti and Liberia, and by your Proclamation, issued on the first day of this year, and the plans you have laid before Congress, you have opened the gates of freedom to the millions of our negro brothers who have been deprived of their manhood by the infernal laws which have so long disgraced the civilization of America.

"We believe that the endeavors already made by you are only intimations of your earnest intentions to carry out to completion the grand and holy work you have begun, and we pray you to go on unfalteringly, undauntedly, never pausing until the vivifying sun of liberty shall warm the blood and inspire the soul of every man who breathes the air of your great Republic. Be assured that, in following out this noble course, our earnest, our active sympathies will be with you, and that, like our brothers in Lancashire, whose distress called forth your generous help in this your own time of difficulty, we would rather perish than band ourselves in unholy alliance with the South and slavery.

"May you and your compatriots be crowned with victory; and may the future see the people of England and their brothers of America marching shoulder to shoulder determinedly forward, the pioneers of human progress, the champions of universal liberty."

A vote of thanks to the chairman brought the proceedings to a close.

SPEECH AT THE LONDON TAVERN,

JUNE 16, 1863.

On the evening of June 16, 1863, a densely crowded public meeting, under the auspices of the Emancipation Society, was held at the London Tavern, to hear from M. D. Conway, Esq., of Eastern Virginia, an address on the war in America. Mr. Bright, M. P., presided.

Mr. Bright spoke as follows: —

I presume that, from the advertisements by which the meeting has been convened, you are, as I am, acquainted with the fact, that the principal object of the meeting is not to listen to me, but to a gentleman whose claim upon your attention is such as no Englishman can pretend to have in connection with the question which is before us to-night. Mr. Conway, who will address you when I sit down, is not an Englishman, but an American; and he is not only an American, but he is of the State of Virginia; and he is not only of the State of Virginia, but he is of one of the eminent families of that State, connected as it has been, unhappily, with an institution which just now forms the great subject of controversy in the United States.

I shall not undertake, in the presence of Mr. Conway, to say what might be interesting to you to hear, and truthful for me to utter in his praise; but I will read an extract from a letter which was written by William Lloyd Garrison, — (cheers,) — the apostle of abolition in the United States, to my friend, George Thompson, — (cheers,) — the apostle of abolition in England. (Hear! Hear!) The letter is dated —

"BOSTON, April 10th, 1863.

"You are such an attentive reader of the *Liberator* and the *Standard*, that the name and services of the bearer of this, Mr. Moncure D. Conway, author of 'The Golden Hour' and 'The Rejected Stone,' &c., must be familiar to you, so that he will need no special introduction. Allied by birth and relationship to the first families in Virginia, the son of a prominent slaveholder, brought up in the midst of slavery and all its pernicious influences, classically educated, he has for several years past been the brave, outspoken, fervid advocate of the Antislavery cause, bringing to it all of Southern fire, resolution, energy, and persistency; and consequently has made himself an exile from his native home and Commonwealth for an indefinite period, though as true to the honor, safety, wealth, and progress of Virginia 'as the needle to the pole.' You well know how to appreciate such a moral hero, and he will rejoice to make your personal acquaintance.

"WILLIAM LLOYD GARRISON."

If I might add one other sentence with regard to Mr. Conway, I should tell you the sad and distressing fact, presented ever to his own mind and memory, that his father, and I believe two of his brothers, and almost all the men of his blood relationship, are at this moment in the Southern armies. I need not, therefore, tell you the depth and the strength of the conviction against slavery which could have led him to the line of conduct which he has pursued for many years past with regard to that question. (Cheers.)

I come then with you to listen to Mr. Conway; but before I give place to him, perhaps I shall not trespass beyond my duty in making some observations upon the subject which now occupies the attention of all men in this country. (Loud cheers.)

If we look back a little over two years,—two years and a half,—when the question of secession was first raised in a practical shape, I think we shall be able to remember that, when the news first arrived in England, there was but one opinion with regard to it,—that every man condemned the folly and the wickedness of the South,—(Hear! Hear!)—and protested against their plea that they had any just grievance which justified them in revolt,—and every man hoped that some mode might be discovered by which the terrible calamity of war might be avoided.

For a time many thought that there would have been no war. Whilst the reins were slipping from the hands — the too feeble hands — of Mr. Buchanan, into the grasp of President Lincoln, — (loud cheers,) — there was a moment when men thought that we were about to see the wonderful example of a great question, which in all other countries would have involved a war, settled perhaps by moderation, — some moderation on one side, and some concession on the other; and so long as men believed that there would be no war, so long everybody condemned the South. We were afraid of a war in America, because we knew that one of the great industries of our country depended upon the continuous reception of its raw material from the Southern States. But it was a folly — it was a gross absurdity — for any man to believe, with the history of the world before him, that the people of the Northern States, twenty millions, with their free government, would for one moment sit down satisfied with the dismemberment of their country, and make no answer to the war which had been commenced by the South. (Great cheering.)

I speak not in justification of war. I am only treating this question upon principles which are almost universally acknowledged throughout the world, and by an overwhelming majority even of those men who accept the Christian religion, — and it is only upon those principles, so almost universally acknowledged, and acknowledged as much in this country as anywhere else, — it is only just that we should judge the United States upon the principles upon which we in this country would be likely to act.

But the North did not yield to the dismemberment of their country, and they did not allow a conspiracy of Southern politicians and slaveholders to seize their forts and arsenals without preparing for resistance; and then, when the people of England found that the North were about to resist, and the war was inevitable, they turned their eyes from the South, which was the beginner of the war, and looked to the North, saying that, if the North would not resist, there could be no war, — (laughter,) — and that we should get our cotton, and trade would go on as before; and therefore, from that hour to this, not a few persons in this country, who at first condemned the South, have been incessant in their condemnation of the North.

Now, I believe this is a fair statement of the feeling which prevailed when the first news of secession arrived, and of the change of opinion which took place in a few weeks, when it was found that, by the resolution of the North to maintain the integrity of their country, war, and civil war, was unavoidable. The trade interests of the country affected our opinion; and I fear did then prevent, and has since prevented, our doing justice to the people of the North. (Hear! Hear! and cheers.)

Now I am going to transport you, in mind, to Lancashire, and the interests of Lancashire, which, after all, are the interests of the whole United Kingdom, and clearly of not a few in this metropolis. Now, what was the condition of our greatest manufacturing industry before the war, and before secession had been practically attempted? It was this: that almost ninety per cent of all our cotton came from the Southern States of the American Union, and was, at least nine tenths of it, the produce of the uncompensated labor of the negro.

Everybody knew that we were carrying on a prodigious industry upon a most insecure foundation; and it was the commonest thing in the world for men who were discussing the present and the future of the cotton trade, whether in Parliament or out of it, to point to the existence of slavery in the United States of America as the dangerous thing in connection with that great trade; and it was one of the reasons which stimulated me on several occasions to urge upon the government of this country to improve the government of India, — (cheers,) — and to give us a chance of receiving a considerable portion of our supply from India, so that we might not be left in absolute want when the calamity occurred, which all thoughtful men knew must some day come, in the United States.

Now, I maintain that with your supply of cotton mainly from the Southern States, raised by slave labor, two things are indisputable: first, that your supply must always be insufficient; and second, that it must always be insecure. Perhaps many of you are not aware that in the United States — I am speaking of the Slave States, and the cotton-growing States — the quantity of land which is cultivated in cotton is a mere garden, a mere plot, in comparison with the whole of the cotton region. I speak from the authority of a report lately presented to the Boston Chamber of Commerce, containing much important information on this question; and I believe that the whole acreage, or the whole breadth of the land on which cotton is grown in America, does not exceed ten thousand square miles, — that is, a space one hundred miles long and one hundred miles broad, or the size of two of our largest counties in England; but the land of the ten chief cotton-producing States is sixty times as much as that, being, I believe, about twelve times the size of England and Wales.

It cannot be, therefore, because there has not been land enough that we have not in former years had cotton enough; it cannot be that there has not been a demand for the produce of the land, for the demand has constantly outstripped the supply; it has not been because the price has not been sufficient, for, as is well known, the price has been much higher of late years, and the profit to the planter much greater; and yet, notwithstanding the land and the demand, and the price, and the profit, the supply of cotton has not been sufficient for the wants of the spinners and the manufacturers of the world, and for the wants of civilization.

The particular facts with regard to this I need not, perhaps, enter into; but I find, if I compare the prices of cotton in Liverpool from 1856 to 1860 with the prices from 1841 to 1845, that every pound of cotton from America and sold in Liverpool fetched in the last five years more than twenty per cent more than it did in the former five years, notwithstanding that we were every year in greater difficulties through finding our supply of cotton insufficient.

Now, what was the reason that we did not get enough? It was because there was not labor enough in the Southern States. You see every day in the newspapers that there are four millions of slaves, but of those four millions of slaves some are growing tobacco, some rice, and some sugar; a very large number are employed in domestic servitude, and a large number in factories, mechanical operations, and business in towns; and there remain only about one million negroes, or only one quarter of the whole number, who are regularly engaged in the cultivation of cotton.

Now, you will see that the production of cotton and its continued increase must depend upon the constantly increasing productiveness of the labor of those one million of negroes, and on the natural increase of population from them. Well, the increase of the population of the slaves in the United States is rather less than two and a half per cent per annum, and the increase on the million will be about twenty-five thousand a year; and the increased production of cotton from that increased amount of labor consisting of twenty-five thousand more negroes every year will probably never exceed — I believe it has not reached — one hundred and fifty thousand bales per annum. The exact facts with regard to this are these: that in the ten years from 1841 to 1850 the average crop was 2,173,000 bales, and in the ten years from 1851 to 1860 it was 3,252,000, being an increase of 1,079,000 bales in the ten years, or only about 100,000 bales of increase per annum.

Now, I think I have shown that the increase of production must depend upon the increase of labor, because every other element is in abundance, — soil, climate, and so forth. (A Voice: "How about sugar?") A gentleman asks about sugar. If in any particular year there was an extravagant profit upon cotton, there might be, and there probably would be, some abstraction of labor from the cultivation of tobacco, and rice, and sugar, in order to apply it to cotton, and a larger temporary increase of growth might take place; but I have given you the facts with regard to the last twenty years, and I think you will see that my statement is correct. (Cheers.)

Now, can this be remedied under slavery? (No! No!) I will show you how it cannot. And first of all, everybody who is acquainted with American affairs knows that there is not very much migration of the population of the Northern States into the Southern States to engage in the ordinary occupations of agricultural labor. Labor is not honorable and is not honored in the South, — (Hear! Hear!) — and therefore free laborers from the North are not likely to go South. Again, of all the emigration from this country, — amounting, as it did, in the fifteen years from 1846 to 1860, to two million five hundred thousand persons, being equal to the whole of the population of this great city, — a mere trifle went South and settled there to pursue the occupation of agriculture; they remained in the North, where labor is honorable and honored.

Whence, then, could the planters of the South receive their increasing labor? Only from the slave-ship and the coast of Africa. But, fortunately for the world, the United States government has never yet become so prostrate under the heel of the slave-owner as to consent to the reopening of the slave-trade. (Loud cheers.) Therefore the Southern planter was in this unfortunate position: he could not tempt, perhaps he did not want, free laborers from the North; he could not tempt, perhaps he did not want, free laborers from Europe; and if he did want, he was not permitted to fetch slave labor from Africa. Well, that being so, we arrive at this conclusion, — that whilst the cultivation of cotton was performed by slave labor, you were shut up for your hope of increased growth to the small increase that was possible with the increase of two and a half per cent per annum in the population of the slaves, about one million in number, that have been regularly employed in the cultivation of cotton.

Then, if the growth was thus insufficient, — and I as one connected with the trade can speak very clearly upon that point, — (Hear! Hear!) — I ask you whether the production and the supply were not necessarily insecure by reason of the institution of slavery? It was perilous with the Union. In this country we made one mistake in our forecast of this question; we did not believe that the South would commit suicide; we thought it possible that the slaves might revolt. They might revolt, but their subjugation was inevitable, because the whole power of the Union was pledged to the maintenance of order in every part of its dominions.

But if there be men who think that the cotton trade would be safer if the South were an independent state, with slavery established there in permanence, these greatly mistake, — (Hear! Hear!) — because whatever was the danger of revolt in the Southern States whilst the Union was complete, the possibility of revolt and the possibility of success would be surely greatly increased, if the North were separate from the South, and the negro had only his Southern master, and not the Northern power, to contend against. (Cheers.)

But I believe there is little danger of revolt, and no possibility of success. When the revolt took place in the island of St. Domingo, the blacks were far superior in numbers to the whites. In the Southern States it is not so, and ignorant, degraded, without organization, without arms, and scarcely with any faint hope of freedom forever, except the enthusiastic one which they have when they believe that God will some day stretch out his arm for their deliverance,—(loud cheers,)—I say that, under these circumstances, to my mind, there was no reasonable expectation of revolt, and there was no expectation whatever of success in any attempt to gain their liberty by force of arms.

But now we are in a different position. Slavery itself has chosen its own issue, and has chosen its own field. Slavery—and when I say slavery, I mean the slave power—has not trusted to the future; but it has rushed into the battle-field to settle this great question; and having chosen war, it is from day to day sinking to inevitable ruin under it. (Cheers.) Now, if we are agreed—and I am keeping you still to Lancashire and to its interests for a moment longer — that this vast industry, with all its interests of capital and labor, has been standing on a menacing volcano, is it not possible that hereafter it may be placed upon a rock which nothing can disturb? (Cheers.)

Imagine, what of course some people will say one has no right to imagine, — imagine the war over, the Union restored, — (Hear! Hear!) — and slavery abolished, — (cheers,) — does any man suppose that there would be in the South one single negro fewer than there are at present? On the contrary, I believe there would be more. I believe there is many a negro in the Northern States, and even in Canada, who, if the lash, and the chain, and the branding-iron, and the despotism against which even he dared not complain, were abolished forever, would turn his face to the sunny lands of the South, and would find himself happier and more useful there than he can be in a more northern clime.

More than this, there would be a migration from the North to the South. You do not suppose that those beautiful States, those regions than which earth offers nothing to man more fertile and more lovely, are shunned by the enterprising population of the North because they like the rigors of a Northern winter and the greater changeableness of the Northern seasons? Once abolish slavery in the South, and the whole of the country will be open to the enterprise and to the industry of all. (Cheers.) And more than that, when you find that, only the other day, not fewer than four thousand emigrants, most of them from the United Kingdom, landed in one day in the city of New York, do you suppose that all those men would go north and west at once? Would not some of them turn their faces southward, and seek the clime of the sun, which is so grateful to all men, and where they would find a soil more fertile, rivers more abundant, and everything that Nature offers more profusely given, but from which they are now shut out by the accursed power which slavery exerts? (Cheers.) Why, with freedom you would have a gradual filling up of the wildernesses of the Southern States; you would have there, not population only, but capital, and industry, and roads, and schools, and everything which tends to produce growth, and wealth, and prosperity. (Loud applause.)

Now, I maintain — and I believe my opinion will be supported by all those men who are most conversant with American affairs — that, with slavery abolished, with freedom firmly established in the South, you would find in ten years to come a rapid increase in the growth of cotton; and not only would its growth be rapid, but its permanent increase would be secure.

I said that I was interested in this great question of cotton. I come from the midst of the great cotton industry of Lancashire; much the largest portion of anything I have in the world depends upon it; not a little of it is now utterly valueless, under the continuance of this war. My neighbors by thousands and scores of thousands are suffering, more or less, as I am suffering; and many of them, as you know, — more than a quarter of a million of them, — have been driven from a subsistence gained by their honorable labor to the extremest poverty, and to a dependence upon the charity of their fellow-countrymen. My interest is the interest of all the population.

My interest is against a mere enthusiasm, a mere sentiment, a mere visionary fancy of freedom as against slavery. I am speaking now as a matter of business. I am glad when matters of business go straight with matters of high sentiment and morality, — (Hear! Hear!) — but from this platform I declare my solemn conviction that there is no greater enemy to Lancashire, to its capital and to its labor, than the man who wishes the cotton agriculture of the Southern States to be continued under slave labor. (Loud cheers.)

Now, one word more upon another branch of the question, and I have done. I would turn for a moment from commerce to politics. I believe that our true commercial interests in this country are very much in harmony with what I think ought to be our true political sympathies. There is no people in the world, I think, that more fully and entirely accepts the theory that one nation acts very much upon the character and upon the career of another, than England; for our newspapers and our statesmen, our writers and our speakers of every class, are constantly telling us of the wonderful influence which English constitutional government and English freedom have on the position and career of every nation in Europe. I am not about to deny that some such influence, and occasionally, I believe, a beneficent influence, is thus exerted; but if we exert any influence upon Europe, — and we pride ourselves upon it, — perhaps it will not be a humiliation to admit that we feel some influence exerted upon us by the great American Republic. American freedom acts upon England, and there is nothing that is better known, at the west end of this great city, — (Hear! Hear!) — from which I have just come, — than the influence that has been, and nothing more feared than the influence that may be, exerted by the United States upon this country.

I left the House of Commons at seven o'clock, about to proceed to what is called a discussion on the ballot. ("Hear! Hear!" and laughter.) There is not generally much discussion, because the whole question really is conceded; there is no practical argument to be made against the ballot, — (Hear! Hear!) — or, if there be a practical argument, it is one that the opponents of the ballot dare not use. (Cheers.) But if you see in the United States that in the elections which took place a few months ago in several States, under the ballot, returns were made which were very hostile to the existing government, and that the popular will was freely expressed, and expressed in the face of a government that has six hundred thousand or eight hundred thousand men in the field, — and if you use that as an argument here, — they wish that the United States were so far off that we could not hear anything about them, because it might unhappily come to pass that the people of England should think that that which saved voters in America from the fear of individual oppression, or, if such a thing were there possible, from the fear of government dictation, might have precisely the same, and an equally beneficial effect, if applied in this country. (Cheers.)

We all of us know that there has been a great effect produced in England by the career of the United States. An emigration of three millions or four millions of persons from the United Kingdom, during the last forty years, has bound us to them by hundreds and thousands of family ties, — (Hear! Hear!) — and therefore it follows that whatever there is that is good, and whatever there is that is free, that we have not, we know something about it, and gradually may begin to wish for, and some day may insist upon having. (Loud cheers.)

And when I speak of "us," I mean the people of this country. When I am asserting this fact that the people of England have a great interest in the well-being of the American Republic, I mean the people of England. I do not speak of the wearers of crowns or of coronets in matters of this kind, —(Hear! Hear!)—but of the twenty millions of people in this country who live on their labor, and who, having no votes, are not counted in our political census, but without whom there could be no British nation at all. (Loud cheers.) I say that these have an interest, almost as great and direct as though they were living in Massachusetts or New York, in the tremendous struggle for freedom which is now shaking the whole Northern population. (Cheers.)

During the last two years there has been much said, and much written, and some things done in this country, which are calculated to gain us the hate of both sections of the American Union. I believe that a course of policy might have been taken by the English press, and by the English government, and by what are called the influential classes in England, that would have bound them to our hearts and to their hearts. I speak of the twenty millions of the Free North. I believe we might have been so thoroughly united with the people, that all remembrance of the war of the Revolution and of the war of 1812 would have been obliterated, and we should have been in heart and spirit for all time forth but one nation.

I can only hope that, as time passes, and our people become better informed, — (Hear! Hear!) — they will be more just, and that ill-feeling of every kind will pass away; that in future all that love freedom here will hold converse with all that love freedom there, and that the two nations, separated as they are by the ocean, come as they are, notwithstanding, of one stock, may be in future time united in soul, and may make together every possible effort for the advancement of the liberties and the happiness of mankind. (Prolonged and enthusiastic applause.)

SPEECH IN THE HOUSE OF COMMONS,

ON MR. ROEBUCK'S MOTION FOR RECOGNITION OF THE SOUTHERN CONFEDERACY,

JUNE 30, 1863.

MR. BRIGHT said: — I will not attempt to follow the noble lord in the labored attack which he has made upon the treasury bench, for these two reasons: that he did not appear to me very much to understand what it was he was charging them with; and, again, I am not in the habit of defending gentlemen who sit on that bench. (Laughter.) I will address myself to the question before the House, which I think the House generally feels to be very important, although I am quite satisfied that they don't feel it to be a practical one. (Hear! Hear!) Neither do I think that the House will be disposed to take any course in support of the honorable gentleman who introduced the resolution now before us. (Hear! Hear!)

We sometimes are engaged in discussions, and have great difficulty to know what we are about; but the honorable gentleman left us in no kind of doubt when he sat down. (Hear! Hear!) He proposed a resolution, in words which, under certain circumstances and addressed to certain parties, might end in offensive or injurious consequences. (Hear! Hear!) Taken in connection with his character — (laughter) — and with the speech he has made to-night, and with the speech he has recently made elsewhere on this subject, I would say that he would have come to about the same conclusion if he proposed to address the Crown inviting the Queen to declare war against the United States of America. (Hear!) The Chancellor of the Exchequer, who is supposed not to be very zealous in the particular line of opinion that I have adopted, — ("Hear! Hear!" and a laugh,) — addressed the honorable gentleman in the smoothest language possible, but still he was obliged to charge him with the tone of bitter hostility which marked his speech. (Hear!)

On a recent occasion the honorable member addressed some members of his constituency, — I don't mean his last speech, I mean the speech in August, last year, — in which he entered upon a course of prophecy which, like most prophecies in our day, does not happen to come true. But he said then what he said to-night, that the American people and government were overbearing. He did not tell them in the least, that the government of the United States had, almost during the whole of his lifetime, been conducted by his friends of the South. He said that, if they were divided, they would not be able to bully the whole world; and he made use of these expressions: "The North will never be our friends; of the South you can make friends, — they are Englishmen, — they are not the scum and refuse of the world." (Hear! Hear!)

Mr. Roebuck: Allow me to correct that statement. What I said I now state to the House, that the men of the South were Englishmen, but that the army of the North was composed of the scum of Europe.

Mr. Bright: I take, of course, that explanation of the honorable and learned gentleman, with this explanation from me, that there is not, so far as I can find, any mention near that paragraph, and I think there is not in the speech a single word, about the army. (Hear! Hear!)

Mr. Roebuck: I assure you I said that.

Mr. Bright: Then I take it for granted that the honorable and learned gentleman said that, or that if he said what I have read he greatly regrets it. ("Hear!" and laughter.)

Mr. Roebuck: No, I did not say it. (Laughter.)

Mr. Bright: The honorable and learned gentleman in his resolution speaks of other powers. Well, he has unceremoniously got rid of all the powers but France, and he comes here to-night with a story of an interview with a man whom he describes as the great ruler of France,—tells us a conversation,—asks us to accept the lead of the Emperor of the French on, I will undertake to say, one of the greatest questions that ever was submitted to the British Parliament. (Cheers.) But it is not long since the honorable and learned gentleman held very different language. (Loud cheers.) I recollect in this House, only about two years ago, that the honorable and learned gentleman said: "I hope I may be permitted to express in respectful terms my opinion, even though it should affect so great a potentate as the Emperor of the French. I have no faith in the Emperor of the French." (Cheers, and laughter.) On another occasion the honorable and learned gentleman said,—not, I believe, in this House,—"I am still of opinion that we have nothing but animosity and bad faith to look for from the

French Emperor." (Laughter, and cheers.) And he went on to say that still, though he had been laughed at, he adopted the patriotic character of "Tear-'em," and was still at his post. (Great laughter.)

Well then, sir, when the honorable and learned gentleman came back, I think from his expedition to Cherbourg, does the House recollect the language he used on that occasion, — language which, if it expressed the sentiments which he felt, at least I think he might have been content to have withheld. If I am not mistaken, referring to the salutation between the Emperor of the French and the Queen of these kingdoms, he said, "When I saw his perjured lips touch that hallowed cheek." (Hear! Hear!) And now, sir, the honorable and learned gentleman has been to Paris, introduced there by the honorable member for Sunderland, — (laughter,) — and he has become as it were in the palace of the French Emperor a co-conspirator with him to drag this country into a policy which

I maintain is as hostile to its interests as it would be degrading to its honor. (Cheers.)

But then the high contracting parties, I suspect, are not agreed, — (a laugh,) — because I will say this in justice to the French Emperor, that there has never come from him in public, nor from any one of his ministers, nor is there anything to be found in what they have written, that is tinctured in the smallest degree with that bitter hostility which the honorable and learned gentleman has constantly exhibited to the United States of America and their people. (Hear! Hear!) France, if not wise in this matter, is at least not unfriendly. The honorable and learned member, in my opinion, — indeed I am sure, — is not friendly, and I believe he is not wise. (Laughter.)

But now, on this subject, without speaking disrespectfully of that great potentate who has taken the honorable and learned gentleman into his confidence, I must say that the Emperor runs the risk of being far too much represented in this House. (Laughter.) We have got two — I will not call them envoys extraordinary, but most extraordinary. (Loud laughter.) And, if report speaks true, even they are not all. The honorable member for King's County (Mr. Hennessy) — I don't see him in his place — came back the other day from Paris, and there were whispers about that he had seen the great ruler of France, and that he could tell everybody in the most confidential manner that the Emperor was ready to make a spring at Russia for the sake of delivering Poland, and that he only waited for a word from the Prime Minister of England. (Laughter and "Hear! Hear!")

Well, I don't understand the policy of the Emperor, if these new ministers of his tell the truth. For, sir, if one gentleman says that he is about to make war with Russia, and another that he is about to make war with America, I am disposed to look at what he is already doing. I find that he is holding Rome against the opinion of all Italy. ("No!" and loud cheers.) He is conquering Mexico by painful steps, every footstep marked by devastation and blood. He is warring, in some desultory manner, it may be, in China, and for aught I know he may be about to do it in Japan. Well, I say that, if he is to engage in dismembering the greatest Eastern Empire and the great Western Republic, he has a greater ambition than Louis XIV., a greater daring than the first of his name; and that, if he endeavors to grasp these great transactions, his dynasty will fall and be buried in the ruins of his own ambition. (Hear! Hear!)

I can say only one sentence upon the question to which the noble lord has directed so much attention. I understand that we have not heard all the story from Paris, and further, that it is not at all remarkable, seeing that the secret has been confided to two persons, that we have not heard it correctly. (Hear! Hear!) I saw my honorable friend, the member for Sunderland, near me, and his face underwent remarkable contortions during the speech of the honorable and learned gentleman, and I felt perfectly satisfied that he did not agree with what his colleague was saying. (Hear! Hear!) I am told there is in existence a little memorandum which contains an account of what was said and done at that interview; and before the discussion closes we shall no doubt have that memorandum produced, and from it know how far those two gentlemen are agreed.

I now come to the proposition which the honorable and learned gentleman has submitted to the House, and which he has already submitted to a meeting of his constituents at Sheffield. At that meeting, on the 27th of May, the honorable and learned gentleman used these words: "What I have to consider is, what are the interests of England: what are for her interests I believe to be for the interests of the world." Now, leaving out of consideration the latter part of that statement, if the honorable and learned gentleman will keep to the first part of it, then what we have now to consider in this question is, what is for the interest of England. But the honorable and learned gentleman has put it in a way to-night almost as offensive as he did before at Sheffield, and has said that the United States would not bully the world if they were divided and subdivided; for he went so far as to contemplate division into more than two independent sections. Well, I say that the whole of the case rests upon a miserable jealousy of the United States, or on what I may term a base fear. (Hear! Hear!) It is a fear which appears to me just as groundless as any of those panics by which the honorable and learned gentleman has helped to frighten the country.

There never was a state in the world which was less capable of aggression with regard to Europe than the United States of America. (Hear! Hear!) I speak of its government, of its confederation, of the peculiarities of its organization; for the House will agree with me, that nothing is more peculiar than the fact of the enormous power which the separate States, both of the North and South, exercise upon the policy and course of the country. I will undertake to say, that, unless in a question of overwhelming magnitude, which would be able to unite any people, it would be utterly hopeless to expect that all the States of the American Union would join together to support the central government in any plan of aggression on England or any other country of Europe. (Hear! Hear!)

Besides, nothing can be more certain than this, that the government which is now in power, and the party which have elected Mr. Lincoln to office, is a moral and peaceable party, which has been above all things anxious to cultivate the best possible state of feeling with regard to England. (Hear! Hear!) The honorable and learned gentleman of all men ought not to entertain this fear of United States aggression, for he is always boasting of his readiness to come into the field himself. ("Hear!" and laughter.) I grant that it would be a great necessity indeed which would justify a conscription in calling out the honorable and learned gentleman, — (loud laughter,) — but I say he ought to consider well before he spreads those alarms among the people. For the sake of this miserable jealousy, and that he may help to break up a friendly nation, he would depart from the usages of nations, and create an everlasting breach between the people of England and the people of the United States of America. (Hear! Hear!) He would do more; and notwithstanding what he has said to-night, I may put this as my strongest argument against his case, — he would throw the weight of England into the scale in favor of the cause of slavery. (Cheers.)

I want to show the honorable and learned

gentleman that England is not interested in the course he proposes we should take; and when I speak of interests, I mean the commercial interests, the political interests, and the moral interests of the country. And first, with regard to the supply of cotton, in which the noble lord, the member for Stamford, takes such a prodigious interest. I must explain to the noble lord that I know a little about cotton. I happen to have been engaged in that business, — not all my life, for the noble lord has seen me here for twenty years, — but my interests have been in it; and at this moment the firm of which I am a member have no less than six mills, which have been at a stand for nearly a year, owing to the impossibility of working under the present conditions of the supply of cotton. I live among a people who live by this trade; and there is no man in England who has a more direct interest in it than I have. Before the war, the supply of cotton was little and costly, and every year it was becoming more costly, for the supply did not keep pace with the demand.

The point that I am going to argue is this: I believe that the war that is now raging in America is more likely to abolish slavery than not, and more likely to abolish it than any other thing that can be proposed in the world. I regret very much that the pride and passion of men are such as to justify me in making this statement. The supply of cotton under slavery must always be insecure. The House felt so in past years; for at my recommendation they appointed a committee, and but for a foolish minister they would have appointed a special commission to India at my request, — (laughter,) — and I feel the more regret that they did not do so. Is there any gentleman in this House who will not agree with me in this, — that it would be far better for our great Lancashire industry that our supply of cotton should be grown by free labor rather than by slave labor? (Hear!)

Before the war, the whole number of negroes engaged in the production of cotton was about one million, — that is, about a fourth of the whole of the negroes in the Slave States. The annual increase in the number of negroes growing cotton was about twenty-five thousand, — only two and a half per cent. It was impossible for the Southern States to keep up their growth of sugar, rice, tobacco, and their ordinary slave productions, and at the same time to increase the growth of cotton more than at a rate corresponding with the annual increase of negroes. Therefore you will find that the quantity of cotton grown, taking ten years together, increased at the rate of about one hundred thousand bales a year. But that was nothing like the quantity which we required. That supply could not be increased, because the South did not cultivate more than probably one and a half per cent of the land which was capable of cultivation for cotton.

The great bulk of the land in the Southern States is uncultivated. Ten thousand square miles are appropriated to the cultivation of cotton; but there are six hundred thousand square miles, or sixty times as much land, which is capable of being cultivated for cotton. It was, however, impossible that that land should be so cultivated, because, although you had climate and sun, you had not labor. The institution of slavery forbade free-labor men in the North to come to the South; and every emigrant that landed in New York from Europe knew that the Slave States were no States for him, and therefore he went North or West. The laws of the United States, the sentiments of Europe and of the world, being against any opening of the slave-trade, the planters of the South were shut up, and the annual increase in the supply of cotton could increase only in the same proportion as the annual increase in the number of their negroes.

There is only one other point with regard to that matter which is worth mentioning.

The honorable and learned gentleman, the member for Sheffield, will understand it, although on some points he seems to be peculiarly dark. (Laughter.) If a planter in the Southern States wanted to grow one thousand bales of cotton a year, he would require about two hundred negroes. Taking them at five hundred dollars, or one hundred pounds each, which is not more than half the price of a first-class hand, the cost of the two hundred would be twenty thousand pounds. To grow one thousand bales of cotton a year you require not only to get hold of an estate, machinery, tools, and other things necessary to carry on the cotton-growing business, but you must find a capital of twenty thousand pounds to buy the actual laborers by whom the plantation is to be worked; and therefore, as every gentleman will see at once, this great trade, to a large extent, was shut up in the hands of men who were required to be richer than would be necessary if slavery did not exist.

Thus the plantation business to a large extent became a monopoly, and therefore even in that direction the production of cotton was constantly limited and controlled. I was speaking to a gentleman the other day from Mississippi. I believe no man in America or in England is more acquainted with the facts of this case. He has been for many years a Senator from the State of Mississippi. He told me that every one of these facts was true, and he said, "I have no doubt whatever that in ten years after freedom in the South, or after freedom in conjunction with the North, the production of cotton would be doubled, and cotton would be forwarded to the consumers of the world at a much less price than we have had it for many years past."

I shall turn for a moment to the political interest, to which the honorable and learned gentleman paid much more attention than to the commercial. The more I consider the course of this war, the more I come to the conclusion that it is improbable in future that the United States will be broken into separate republics. I do not come to the conclusion that the North will conquer the South. But I think the conclusion to which I am more disposed to come now than at any time since the breaking out of the war is this,—that if a separation should occur for a time, still the interest, the sympathies, the sentiments, the necessities of the whole continent, and its ambition also, as honorable gentlemen mentioned, which seems to some people to be a necessity, render it highly probable that the continent would still be united under one central goverment. (Hear!) I may be quite mistaken. I do not express that opinion with any more confidence than honorable gentlemen have expressed theirs in favor of a permanent dissolution; but now is not this possible, — that the Union may be again formed on the basis of the South? There are persons who think that possible. I hope it is not, but we cannot say that it is absolutely impossible.

Is it not possible that the Northern government might be beaten in their military operations? Is it not possible that, by their own incapacity, they might be humiliated before their own people? and is it not even possible that that party which you please to call the Peace party in the North, but which is in no sense a peace party, should unite with the South, and that the Union should be reconstituted on the basis of the Southern opinions and of the Southern social system? Is it not possible, for example, that the Southern people, and those in their favor, should appeal to the Irish population of America against the negroes, between whom there has been little sympathy and little respect, — and is it not possible they should appeal to the commercial classes of the North, — and the rich commercial classes in all countries, who, from the uncertainty of their possessions and the fluctuation of their interests, are rendered always timid and almost always corrupt, — (cheers and laughter,)

— is it not possible, I say, that they might prefer the union of their whole country upon the basis of the South, rather than that union which many members of this House look upon with so much apprehension ?

If that should ever take place, — but I believe, with my honorable friend below me, (Mr. Forster,) in the moral government of the world, and therefore I cannot believe that it will take place, — but if it were to take place, with their great armies, and with their great navy, and their almost unlimited power, they might offer to drive England out of Canada, France out of Mexico, and whatever nations are interested in them out of the islands of the West Indies; and you might then have a great state built upon slavery and war, instead of that free state to which I look, built up upon an educated people, upon general freedom, and upon morality in government. (Loud cheers.)

Now there is one more point to which the honorable and learned gentleman will forgive me if I allude, — he does not appear to me to think it of great importance, — and that is, the morality of this question. The right honorable gentleman, the Chancellor of the Exchequer, and the honorable gentleman who spoke from the bench behind, — and I think the noble lord, if I am not mistaken, — referred to the carnage which is occasioned by this lamentable strife. (Hear! Hear!) Well, carnage, I presume, is the accompaniment of all war. Two years ago the press of London laughed very much — if I may use such a term of the newspapers — at the battles of the United States, in which nobody was killed and few were hurt. There was a time when I stood up in this House, and pointed out the dreadful horrors of war. (An ironical cheer.) There was a war waged by this country in the Crimea; and the Chancellor of the Exchequer, with an uneasy conscience, is constantly striving to defend that struggle. That war — for it lasted about the same time that the American war has lasted — at least destroyed as many lives as are estimated to have been destroyed in the United States. ("Hear! Hear!" and "No! No!")

My honorable friend, the member for Montrose, — who, I think, is not in the House, — made a speech in Scotland some time last year, in which he gave the numbers which were lost by Russia in that war. (Hear! Hear!) An honorable friend near me observes, that some people don't reckon the Russians for anything. (Hear! Hear!) I say, if you will add the Russians to the English, and the two to the French, and the three to the Sardinians, and the four to the Turks, that more lives were lost in the invasion of the Crimea, in the two years that it lasted, than have been lost now in the American war. (Cries of "Hear! Hear!") That is no defence of the carnage of the American war at all; but let honorable gentlemen bear in mind that, when I protested against the carnage in the Crimea, — for an object which few could comprehend and nobody can fairly explain, — I was told that I was actuated by a morbid sentimentality. Well, if I was converted, and if I view the mortality in war with less horror than I did then, it must be attributed to the arguments of honorable gentlemen opposite, and on the Treasury bench; but the fact is, I view this carnage just as I viewed that, with only this difference, that while our soldiers perished three thousand miles from home in a worthless and indefensible cause, these men were on their own soil, and every man of them knew for what he enlisted and for what purpose he was to fight. (Hear! Hear!)

Now, I will ask the right honorable gentleman, the Chancellor of the Exchequer, and those who are of opinion with him on this question of slaughter in the American war, — a slaughter which I hope there is no honorable member here, and no person out of this House, that does not in his calm moments look upon with grief and horror, —

(Hear! Hear!) — to consider what was the state of things before the war. It was this, — that every year in the Slave States of America there were one hundred and fifty thousand children born into the world, — born with the badge and the doom of slavery, — born to the liability by law, and by custom, and by the devilish cupidity of man, — ("Oh! Oh!" and loud cheers,) — to the lash and to the chain and to the branding-iron, and to be taken from their families and carried they know not where. (Loud cheers.)

I want to know whether you feel as I feel upon this question. When I can get down to my home from this House, I find half a dozen little children playing upon my hearth. (Cheers and laughter.) How many members are there who can say with me, that the most innocent, the most pure, the most holy joy which in their past years they have felt, or in their future years they have hoped for, has not arisen from contact and association with our precious children? (Loud cheers.) Well, then, if that be so, — if, when the hand of death takes one of those flowers from our dwelling, our heart is overwhelmed with sorrow and our household is covered with gloom, — what would it be if our children were brought up to this infernal system, — one hundred and fifty thousand of them every year brought into the world in these Slave States, amongst these "gentlemen," amongst this "chivalry," amongst these men that we can make our friends.

Do you forget the thousand-fold griefs and the countless agonies which belonged to the silent conflict of slavery before the war began? ("Hear! Hear!" and cheers.) It is all very well for the honorable and learned gentleman to tell me, to tell this House, — he won't tell the country with any satisfaction to it, — that slavery, after all, is not so bad a thing. The brother of my honorable friend, the member for South Durham, told me that in North Carolina he himself saw a woman whose every child, ten in number, had been sold when they grew up to that age at which they would fetch a price to their master. (Cheers.)

I have not heard a word to-night of another question, — which is the Proclamation of the President of the United States. The honorable and learned gentleman spoke somewhere in the country, and he had not the magnanimity to abstain from a statement which I was going to say he must have known had no real weight. I can make all allowance for the passion, — and I was going to say the malice, — but I will say the ill-will of the honorable and learned gentleman; but I make no allowance for his ignorance. I make no allowance for that, because if he is ignorant it is his own fault, for God has given him an intellect which ought to keep him from ignorance on a question of this magnitude. I now take that Proclamation. What do you propose to do? You propose by your resolution, to help the South, if possible, to gain and sustain its independence. (Hear!)

Nobody doubts that. The honorable and learned gentleman will not deny it. But what becomes of the Proclamation? I should like to ask any lawyer in what light we stand as regards that Proclamation? To us there is only one country in what was called the United States, — there is only one President, — there is only one general Legislature, there is only one law; and if that Proclamation be lawful anywhere, — ("Hear!" from Mr. Roebuck,) — we are not in a condition to deny its legality, because at present we know no President Davis, nor do we know the men who are about him. We have our consuls in the South, but recognizing only one Legislature, one President, one law. So far as we are concerned, that Proclamation is a legal and effective document.

I want to know, to ask you, the House of Commons, whether you have turned back to your own proceedings in 1834, and traced the praises which have been lavished upon you for thirty years by the great and good men of other countries,—(cheers,)—and whether, after what you did at that time, you believe that you will meet the views of the thoughtful, moral, and religious people of England, when you propose to remit to slavery three millions of negroes in the Southern States, who in our views, and regarding the Proclamation of the only President of the United States as a legal document, are certainly and to all intents and purposes free. ("Oh!") The honorable and learned gentleman may say "Oh!" and shake his head lightly, and chuckle at this. He has managed to get rid of all those feelings under which all men, black and white, like to be free. He has talked of the cant and hypocrisy of these men. Was Wilberforce, was Clarkson, was Buxton,—I might run over the whole list,—were these men hypocrites, and had they nothing about them but cant? (Cheers.)

I could state something about the family of my honorable friend below me (Mr. Forster), which I almost fear to state in his presence; but his reverend father — a man unsurpassed in character, not equalled by many in intellect, and approached by few in service — laid down his life in a Slave State in America, while carrying to the governors and legislatures of every Slave State the protest of himself and his sect against the enormity of that odious system.

In conclusion, sir, I have only this to say, — that I wish to take of this question a generous view, — a view, I say, generous with regard to the people with whom we are in amity, whose Minister we receive here, and who receive our Minister in Washington. We see that the government of the United States has for two years past been contending for its life, and we know that it is contending necessarily for human freedom. That government affords the remarkable example — offered for the first time in the history of the world — of a great government coming forward as the organized defender of law, freedom, and equality. ("Oh!" and cheers.)

Surely honorable gentlemen opposite cannot be so ill-informed as to say, that the revolt of the Southern States is in favor of freedom and equality. In Europe often, and in some parts of America, when there has been insurrection, it has been of the suffering generally against the oppressor, and rarely has it been found, and not more commonly in our history than in the history of any other country, that the government has stepped forward as the organized defender of freedom, — of the wide and general freedom of those under their rule. With such a government, in such a contest, with such a foe, the honorable and learned gentleman, the member for Sheffield, who professes to be more an Englishman than most Englishmen, asks us to throw into the scale against them the weight of the hostility of England.

I have not said a word with regard to what may happen to England if we go into war with the United States. It will be a war on the ocean, — every ship that belongs to the two nations will, as far as possible, be swept from the seas; but when the troubles in America are over, — be they ended by restoration of the Union, or by separation, — that great and free people, the most instructed in the world, — (loud cries of "No!") — there is not an American to be found in the New England States who cannot read and write, and there are not three men in one hundred in the whole Northern States who cannot read and write, — (cheers,) — and those who cannot read and write are those who have recently come from Europe, — (laughter,) — I say the most instructed people in the world, and the most wealthy, — if you take the distribution of wealth among the whole people, — you will leave in their hearts a wound which probably a century may not heal, and the posterity of some of those who now hear my voice may look back with amazement, and I will say with lamentation, at the course which was taken by the honorable and learned gentleman, and by such honorable members as may choose to follow his leading. (No! No!) I suppose the honorable gentlemen who cry "No!" will admit that we sometimes suffer from some errors of our ancestors. (Hear! Hear!) There are few persons who will not admit that, if their fathers had been wiser, their children would have been happier. (Hear! Hear!)

We know the cause of this revolt, its purposes, and its aims. (Hear!) Those who made it have not left us in darkness respecting their intentions, — (Hear! Hear!) — but what they are to accomplish is still hidden from our sight; and I will abstain now, as I have always abstained with regard to it, from predicting what is to come. (Hear! Hear!) I know what I hope for, — and what I shall rejoice in, — but I know nothing of future facts that will enable me to express a confident opinion. (Hear! Hear!) Whether it will give freedom to the race which white men have trampled in the dust, or whether the issue will purify a nation steeped in crime in connection with its conduct to that race, is known only to the Supreme. (Hear! Hear!) In His hands are alike the breath of man and the life of states. I am willing to commit to Him the issue of this dreaded contest; but I implore of Him, and I beseech this House, that my country may lift nor hand nor voice in aid of the most stupendous act of guilt that history has recorded in the annals of mankind. (Loud cheers, amidst which the honorable gentleman resumed his seat.)

CONCLUSION OF A SPEECH AT A MEETING AT ROCHDALE,

NOVEMBER 24, 1863.

This Meeting was held to enable Mr. Cobden to meet his Constituents, and Mr. Bright, as one of his Constituents, was present at it.

AFTER speaking on the question of Parliamentary Reform, Mr. BRIGHT said:—

But there is one point of this question to which I must refer before I sit down, and that is, that the enemies of popular right and power have been pointing everybody to the dreadful proof which is afforded in America, that an extended suffrage is to be shunned as the most calamitous thing possible to a country.

Now I must refer to the speeches that have dealt with this question in this manner, or to newspapers which have so treated it. I believe now that a great many people in this country are beginning to see that those who have been misleading them for the last two or three years have been either profoundly dishonest or profoundly ignorant. (Cheers.) If I am to give my opinion upon it, I should say that that which has taken place in America within the last three years affords the most triumphant answer to the charges of this kind. Now let us see the government of the United States. We will speak now, — I might say a good deal in favor of the States of the South even, — but we will speak of the Free States in the North; they have a suffrage that you almost call here a manhood suffrage; there are frequent elections, vote by ballot, and ten, twenty, and a hundred thousand vote at an election.

Well, will anybody deny now that the government at Washington, as regards its own people, is the strongest government in the world, at this hour? (Cheers.) And for this simple reason, that it is based on the will, and the good-will, of an instructed people. (Cheers.) Look at its power. I am not now discussing why it is, or the cause which is developing this power, but power is the thing which men regard in these old countries, and which they ascribe mainly to these European institutions. But look at the power which the United States have developed. They have brought more men into the field, built more ships for their navy, they have shown greater resources, than any nation in Europe is capable of. Look at the order which has prevailed. Their elections, at which, as you see by the papers, fifty thousand, or one hundred thousand, or a quarter of a million persons voted, in a given State, are conducted with less disorder than you have seen lately in three of the smallest boroughs in England, — (Hear!) — Barnstaple, Windsor, and Andover. (Laughter and cheers.) Look at their industry. Notwithstanding this terrific struggle, their agriculture, their manufactures and commerce, proceed with an uninterrupted success, and they are ruled by a President, not chosen, it is true, from some worn-out royal or noble blood, — (Hear!) — but from the people, and whose truthfulness and spotless honor have gained him universal praise. (Loud cheers.)

The country that has been vilified through half the organs of the press in England during the last three years, and has been pointed out, too, as an example to be shunned by many of your statesmen, — that country, now in mortal strife, affords a haven and a home for multitudes flying from the burdens and the neglect of the old governments of Europe. (Cheers.) And when this mortal strife is over, when peace is restored, when slavery is destroyed, when the Union is cemented afresh, — for I would say, in the language of one of her own poets, addressing his country,

> "The grave 's not dug where traitor hands shall lay
> In fearful haste thy murdered corse away," —

(loud cheers,) — then Europe and England

may learn that an instructed democracy is the surest foundation of government, and that education and freedom are the only sources of true greatness and true happiness among any people.

EXTRACT FROM A SPEECH AT THE TOWN-HALL, BIRMINGHAM,

JANUARY 26, 1864.

Mr. Bright said:—There is one other question to which my honorable colleague has devoted a considerable portion of his speech. He said, and I believe it, that a year ago he felt it a painful thing to stand here to avow opinions contrary to those of many of his friends, and contrary to those which I had avowed before. Well, I told you then how painful a thing it was for me to stand up and to controvert on this platform any of the statements which he had made.

I came here to-night intending to say no single word as to the question between North and South in the United States. My opinion is, that the unanimous judgment of the people of England, so far as that is ever shown upon any public question, is in favor of the course which her Majesty's government have publicly declared it to be their intention to pursue. (Loud cheers.) I believe that my honorable friend is mistaken in the view he takes of the meaning, and of the result, of what he calls the recognition of the South. (Cheers.) I have seen it stated by authority, North as well as South, and by authority which I may term English, and by authority from France, that, in the present condition of that quarrel, recognition, by all the usages of nations, must necessarily lead to something more. Therefore, although there were no question of slavery, — even though it were simply a political revolt, and there were no special moral question connected with it,—I believe, looking to the past usages of this country with regard to the rebellion of the Greeks against Turkey, and with regard to the revolt of the colonies of South America against Spain, — I am persuaded that it can be demonstrated that those cases afford no support whatever to the argument that we are permitted now to recognize the South, and that, if such recognition did take place now, it could only exasperate still more the terrible strife which exists on the North American continent. (Cheers.)

Now I am myself of opinion, as I have been from the first, that the people of America, so numerous, so powerful, so instructed, so capable in every way, will settle the difficulties of that continent without asking the old countries of Europe to take any share in them. (Cheers.) I believe that, in the providence of the Supreme, the slaveholder, untaught and unteachable by fact or argument or Christian precept, has been permitted to commit, I 'll not call it the crime, but the act of suicide. (Loud cheers.) Whether President Lincoln be in favor of abolition, whether the North are unanimous against slavery, whatever may be said or thought with regard to the transactions on that continent, he must be deaf and blind, and worse than deaf and blind, who does not perceive that, through the instrumentality of this strife, that most odious and most intolerable offence against man and against Heaven, the slavery of the South, — (tremendous cheers,) — the bondage of four millions of our fellow-creatures, is coming to a certain and rapid end. (Renewed cheering.)

Sir, I will say of this question, that I look forward to the time when I shall stand upon this platform with my honorable colleague, and when he will join me, — for he is honest and frank enough to do that, — (cheers,) — when he will join with me in rejoicing that there does not breathe a slave on the North American continent, — (cheers,) — that the Union has been completely restored. (Cheers.) And no less will he rejoice that England did not, in the remotest manner, by a word or breath, or the raising of a finger, do one single thing to promote the atrocious object of the leaders of this accursed insurrection. (Loud cheers.)

SPEECH ON THE CANADIAN FORTIFICATIONS,

DELIVERED IN THE HOUSE OF COMMONS, MARCH 23, 1865.

Mr. Bright remarked: — I shall ask the attention of the House for only a few moments. If the honorable member (Mr. Bentinck) divides, I shall go into the same lobby with him. (Cheers and laughter.) I am afraid that, in making that announcement, I shall excite some little alarm in the mind of the honorable gentleman. (A laugh.) I wish, therefore, to say, that I shall not go into the lobby agreeing with him in many of the statements he has made. The right honorable gentleman (Mr. Disraeli) said, that he approached the military question with great diffidence, and I was very glad to see any signs of diffidence in that quarter. (Much laughter.) After that explanation, he asked the House with a triumphant air whether there is any difficulty in defending a frontier of one thousand or fifteen hundred miles, and whether the practicability of doing so is a new doctrine in warfare. But one thousand or fifteen hundred miles of frontier to defend at the centre of your power, is one thing; but at three thousand or four thousand miles from the centre, it is an entirely different thing. (Hear! Hear!) I venture to say, that there is not a man in this House, or a sensible man out of it, who, apart from the consideration of this vote, or some special circumstances attending it, believes that the people of this country could attempt a successful defence of the frontier of Canada against the whole power of the United States. I said the other night, that I hoped we should not now talk folly, and hereafter, in the endeavor to be consistent, act folly. We all know perfectly well, that we are talking folly when we say that the government of this country would send either ships or men to make an effectual defence of Canada against the power of the United States, supposing war to break out. Understand, I am not in the least a believer in the probability of war, but I will discuss the question for one moment as if war were possible. I suppose some men in this House think it probable. But if it be possible or probable, and if you have to look this difficulty in the face, there is no extrication from it but in the neutrality or independence of Canada.

I agree with those members who say that it is the duty of a great empire to defend every portion of it. I admit that, as a general proposition, though honorable gentlemen opposite, and some on this side, do not apply that rule to the United States. But, admitting that rule, and supposing that we are at all points unprepared for such a catastrophe, may we not, as reasonable men, look ahead, and try if it be not possible to escape from it? (An honorable member, — "Run away?") No, not by running away, though there are many circumstances in which brave men run away; and you may get into difficulty on this Canadian question, which may make you look back and wish that you had run away a good time ago. (Laughter.) I object to this vote on a ground which, I believe, has not been raised by any member in the present discussion. I am not going to say, that the expenditure of fifty thousand pounds is a matter of great consequence to this country, that the expenditure of this money in the proposed way will be taken as a menace by the United States. I do not think that that can be fairly said; for whether building fortifications at Quebec be useless or not, that proceeding is not likely to enable the Canadians to overrun the State of New York. ("Hear!" and a laugh.) The United States, I think will have no right to complain of this expenditure. The utmost it can do will be to show them that some portions, and perhaps the government, of this country have some little distrust of them, and so far it may do injury. I complain of the expenditure and the policy announced by the Colonial Secretary, on a ground which I thought ought to have been urged by the noble lord, the member for Wick, who is a sort of half-Canadian. He made a speech which I listened to with great pleasure, and told the House what some of us, perhaps, did not know before; but if I had been connected, as he is, with Canada, I would have addressed the House from a Canadian point of view.

What is it that the member for Oxford says? He states, in reference to the expenditure for the proposed fortifications, that, though a portion of the expenditure is to be borne by us, the main portion is to be borne by Canada; but I venture to tell him, that, if there shall be any occasion to defend Canada at all, it will not arise from anything Canada does, but from what England does; and therefore I protest against the doctrine that the Cabinet in London may get into difficulties, and ultimately into war, with the Cabinet at Washington, — and because Canada lies adjacent to the United States, and consequently may become the great battle-field, that this United Kingdom has a right to call on Canada for the main portion of that expenditure. (Hear!) Who has asked you to spend fifty thousand pounds, and the hundreds of thousands which may be supposed to follow, but which perhaps Parliament may be indisposed hereafter to grant? What is the proportion which Canada is to bear? If we are to spend two hundred thousand pounds at Quebec, is Canada to spend four hundred thousand pounds at Montreal? If Canada is to spend double of whatever we may spend, is it not obvious that every Canadian will ask himself what is the advantage of the connection between Canada and England?

Every Canadian knows perfectly well, and nobody better than the noble lord the member for Wick, that there is no more prospect of a war between Canada and the United States alone, than between the Empire of France and the Isle of Man; if that is so, why should the Canadians be taxed beyond all reason, as the Colonial Secretary proposes to tax them, for a policy not Canadian, and for a calamity which, if ever it occurs, must occur from some transactions between England and the United States? There are gentlemen here who know a good deal of Canada, and I see behind me one who knows perfectly well what is the condition of the Canadian finances. We complain that Canada levies higher duties on British manufactures than the United States did before the present war, and much higher than France does. But when we complain to Canada of this, and say it is very unpleasant usage from a part of our empire, the Canadians reply that their expenditure is so much, and their debt, with the interest on it, so much, and that they are obliged to levy these heavy duties. If the Canadian finances are in the unfortunate position described,—if the credit of Canada is not very great in the market of this country, and if you see what are the difficulties of the Canadians during a period of peace,—consider what will be their difficulties if the doctrine of the Colonial Secretary be carried out, and that, whatever expenditure is necessary for the defence of Canada, while we bear a portion, the main part must be borne by Canada.

We must then come to the inevitable conclusion, that every Canadian will say, "We are close alongside of a great nation; our parent state is three thousand miles away; there are litigious, and there may be even warlike people, in both nations, and they may occasion the calamity of a great war; we are peaceable people, having no foreign politics, happily; we may be involved in war, and while the great cities of Great Britain are not touched by a single shell, nor one of its fields ravaged, not a city or a village in this Canada in which we live but will be liable to the ravages of war on the part of our powerful neighbor." Therefore the Canadians will say, unless they are unlike all other Englishmen, who appear to have more sense the farther they go from their own country, — (laughter,) — that it would be better for Canada to be disentangled from the politics of England, and to assume the position of an independent state.

I suspect from what has been stated by official gentlemen in the present government, and in previous governments, that there is no objection to the independence of Canada whenever Canada may wish it. I have been glad to hear those statements, because I think they mark an extraordinary progress in sound opinions in this country. I recollect the noble lord at the head of the Foreign Office being very angry in this House at the idea of making a great empire less; but a great empire, territorially, may be lessened without its power and authority in the world being diminished.

(Hear! Hear!) I believe if Canada now, by a friendly separation from this country, became an independent state, choosing its own form of government, — monarchical, if it liked a monarchy, or republican, if it preferred a republic, — it would not be less friendly to England, and its tariff would not be more adverse to our manufactures than now. In the case of a war with America, Canada would then be a neutral country; and the population would be in a state of greater security. Not that I think there is any fear of war, but the government admit that it may occur by their attempt to obtain money for these fortifications. I object, therefore, to this vote, not on that account, nor even because it causes some distrust, or may cause it, in the United States, although that might be some reason; but I object to it mainly because I think we are commencing a policy which we shall either have to abandon, because Canada will not submit to it, or else which will bring upon Canada a burden in the shape of fortification expenditure, that will make her more and more dissatisfied with this country, and that will lead rapidly to her separation from us. I don't object to that separation in the least; I believe it would be better for us, and better for her. But I think that, of all the misfortunes which could happen between us and Canada, this would be the greatest, that her separation should take place after a period of irritation and estrangement, and that we should have on that continent to meet another element in some degree hostile to this country.

I am sorry, sir, that the noble lord at the head of the government, and his colleagues, have taken this course; but it appears to me to be wonderfully like almost everything which the government does. It is a government apparently of two parts, the one part pulling one way and the other part pulling another, and the result generally is something which does not please anybody, or produce any good effect in any direction. ("Hear!

Hear!" and a laugh.) They now propose a scheme which has just enough in it to create distrust and irritation, enough to make it in some degree injurious, and they don't do enough to accomplish any of the objects for which, according to their statements, the proposition is made. (Hear! Hear!) Somebody asked the other night whether the Administration was to rule, or the House of Commons. Well, I suspect from the course of the debates, that on this occasion the Administration will be allowed to rule. We are accustomed to say that the government suggests a thing on its own responsibility, and therefore we will allow them to do it. But the fact is, that the government knows no more of this matter than any other dozen gentlemen in this House. (Hear!) They are not a bit more competent to form an opinion upon it. They throw it down on the table, and ask us to discuss and vote it.

I should be happy to find the House disregarding all the intimations that war is likely, anxious not to urge Canada into incurring an expenditure which she will not bear, and which, if she will not bear, must end in one of two things,—either in throwing of the whole burden upon us, or the breaking up, perhaps suddenly and in anger, of the connection between us and that colony, making our future relations with her most unsatisfactory. I don't place much reliance on the speech of the right honorable member for Buckinghamshire, not because he cannot judge of the question just as well as I or any one of us can do, but because I notice that in matters of this kind gentlemen on that (the Opposition) bench, whatever may have been their animosities towards the gentlemen on this (the Treasury) bench on other questions, shake hands. They may tell you that they have no connection with the House over the way,—(a laugh,)—but the fact is, their connection is most intimate. (Hear! Hear!) And if the right honorable member for Buckinghamshire were now sitting on the Treasury bench, and the noble Viscount were sitting opposite to him, the noble Viscount, I have no doubt, would give him the very same support as he now receives from the right honorable gentleman. (Hear! Hear!)

This seems to me a question so plain, so much on the surface, appealing so much to our common sense, having in it such great issues for the future, that I am persuaded it is the duty of the House of Commons on this occasion to take the matter out of the hands of the executive government, and to determine that, with regard to the future policy of Canada, we will not ourselves expend the money of the English tax-payers, and not force upon the tax-payers of Canada a burden which, I am satisfied, they will not long continue to bear. (Hear! Hear!)

Cambridge: Printed by Welch, Bigelow, & Co.

www.ingramcontent.com/pod-product-compliance
Lightning Source LLC
LaVergne TN
LVHW010214110826
845151LV00004B/1079